21ST Century
Communication 2
LISTENING, SPEAKING, AND CRITICAL THINKING
Second Edition

JESSICA WILLIAMS

RICHARD WALKER

NATIONAL
GEOGRAPHIC
LEARNING

Australia · Brazil · Canada · Mexico · Singapore · United Kingdom · United States

NATIONAL GEOGRAPHIC LEARNING

National Geographic Learning,
a Cengage Company

21st Century Communication 2, **Second Edition**
Jessica Williams and Richard Walker

Publisher: Andrew Robinson

Executive Editor: Sean Bermingham

Senior Development Editor: Melissa Pang

Development Editor: Bettina Liu

Assistant Editor: Dawne Law

Director of Global Marketing: Ian Martin

Heads of Regional Marketing:

   Charlotte Ellis (Europe, Middle East and Africa)

   Justin Kaley (Asia and Greater China)

   Irina Pereyra (Latin America)

   Joy MacFarland (US and Canada)

Product Marketing Manager: Tracy Bailie

Senior Production Controller: Tan Jin Hock

Senior Media Researcher: Leila Hishmeh

Senior Designer: Heather Marshall

Operations Support: Hayley Chwazik-Gee

Manufacturing Buyer: Terrence Isabella

Composition: MPS North America LLC

For permission to use material from this text or product, submit all requests online at **cengage.com/permissions**
Further permissions questions can be emailed to **permissionrequest@cengage.com**

Student's Book with Spark platform access:
ISBN-13: 978-0-357-85598-0

Student's Book:
ISBN-13: 978-0-357-86197-4

National Geographic Learning
200 Pier 4 Boulevard
Boston, MA 02210
USA

Locate your local office at **international.cengage.com/region**

Visit National Geographic Learning online at **ELTNGL.com**
Visit our corporate website at **www.cengage.com**

Printed in Singapore
Print Number: 01 Print Year: 2023

Topics and Featured Speakers

Scope and Sequence

Welcome to *21st Century Communication, Second Edition*

21st Century Communication Listening, Speaking, and Critical Thinking uses big ideas from TED and National Geographic Explorers to look at one topic from different perspectives, present real and effective communication models, and prepare students to share their ideas confidently in English. Each unit develops students' listening, speaking, and critical thinking skills to achieve their academic and personal goals.

Each unit opens with an **impactful photograph** to introduce the topic and act as a springboard for classroom discussion.

Q How should we set realistic life goals?

Everyone makes plans to achieve their goals. Athletes such as Armand Duplantis (pictured at the 2020 World Athletics Indoor Tour), for example, train hard to be the best at their sport. An Olympic champion, Duplantis has broken several world records and aims to continue setting new records in pole vaulting.

What about other goals that we may have in life, such as our career, studies, or health? How can we set ourselves up for success? In this unit, we'll look at different advice and suggestions on how to set achievable goals.

NEW The **Essential Question** outlines the central idea of the unit and directs students' focus to the main topic.

UPDATED Building Vocabulary uses infographics and readings to introduce vocabulary in context and teach words and phrases needed for academic studies.

Big ideas inspire many viewpoints. What's yours?

UPDATED Viewing and Note-taking allows students to explore one aspect of the unit theme and sharpen their academic skills with note-taking and listening comprehension practice.

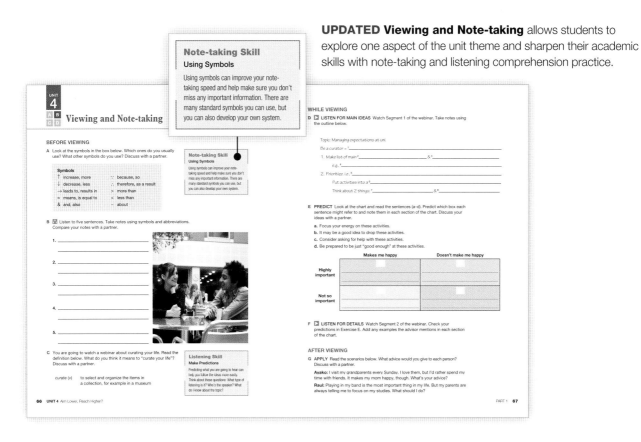

NEW Noticing Language provides students with useful language structures and communication skills to share their ideas confidently.

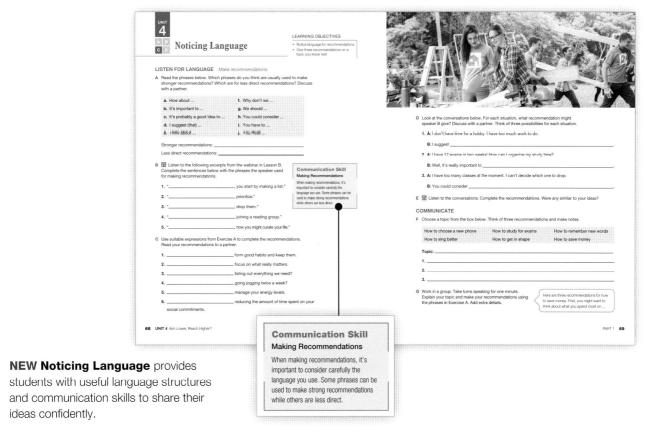

NEW Communicating Ideas encourages students to express their opinions, make decisions, and explore solutions to problems through collaboration.

UPDATED Viewing and Note-taking uses big ideas from TED and National Geographic Explorers to present another aspect of the unit theme and help students improve their academic listening, note-taking skills, and pronunciation.

NEW Thinking Critically gives students a chance to synthesize, analyze, and evaluate the unit's ideas and find their voice in English.

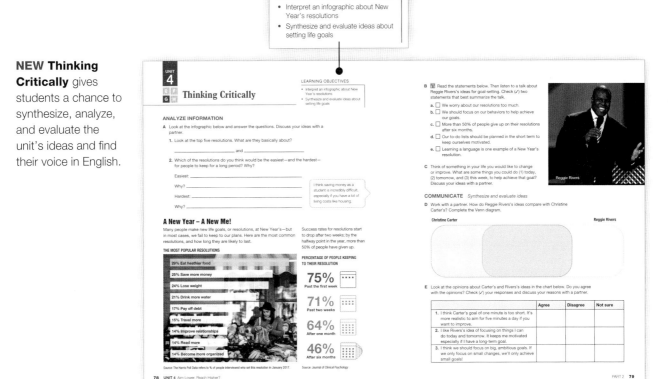

UPDATED Putting It Together has students prepare, plan, and present their ideas clearly and creatively in a final assignment.

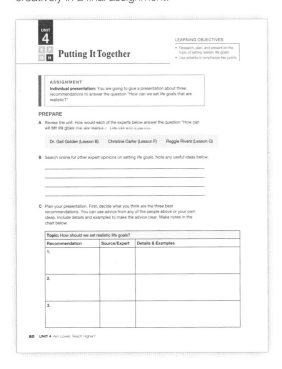

The **Spark** platform delivers your digital tools for every stage of teaching and learning, including auto-graded Online Practice activities, customizable Assessment Suite tests and quizzes, Student's eBook, Classroom Presentation Tool, and downloadable Teacher's Resources.

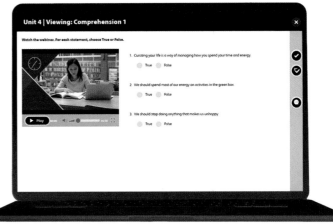

TikTok user Marissa Meizz at a "No More Lonely Friends" event at Central Park in New York, U.S.A. A few hundred people came to her event.

1

Human Connection

Q **How can we form closer bonds?**

We communicate with a lot of people every day, but how strong are our relationships with one another? One TikTok user, Marissa Meizz (pictured), used the power of social media to organize events that help people online make friends in real life. Her "No More Lonely Friends" events have helped hundreds of people connect and make new friends. In this unit, we'll look at some projects that aim to bring people closer together.

THINK and DISCUSS

1 Look at the photo and read the caption. What are the people doing? What kinds of interaction can you see?

2 Look at the essential question and the unit introduction. How do you usually communicate with other people?

Building Vocabulary

LEARN KEY WORDS

A 🎧 Listen to and read the information below. How did Chang bring people in her community together? Was she successful? Discuss with a partner.

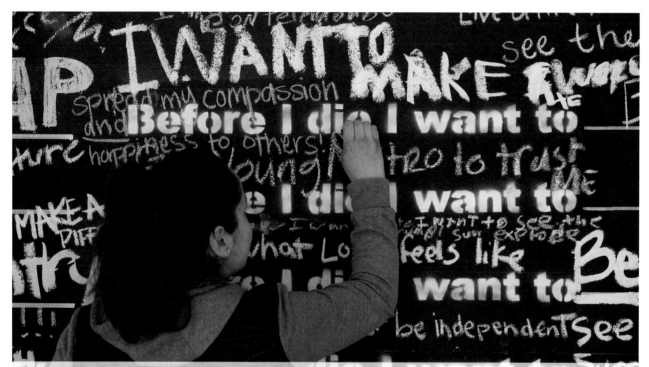

MESSAGE ON A WALL

In 2011, artist Candy Chang started an art project. She wanted to build stronger **connections** among people in her **community**. She wrote one sentence on a wall over and over again: "Before I die, I want to …". She was curious to see how people would **reflect** on their lives and complete the sentence. She also wanted to see whether people would share their **private** feelings and **thoughts** in a public space with **strangers**. Her wall became very popular, and she received hundreds of **responses**. Some of the responses she got were full of hope, but some expressed **anxiety**. Since then, people have created **similar** walls around the world. More than 5,000 "Before I Die" walls have been **created** in over 70 countries and 30 languages.

Source: Chang (2013); Percentage of responses for each topic, based on 100,000 responses from around the world.

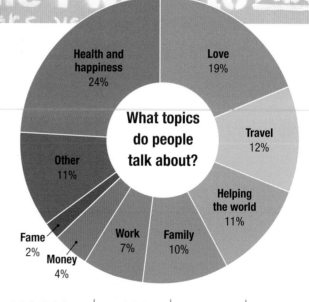

What topics do people talk about?

Health and happiness 24%
Love 19%
Travel 12%
Helping the world 11%
Family 10%
Work 7%
Money 4%
Fame 2%
Other 11%

| 100,000+ responses | 5,000+ walls | 73 countries | 36 languages |

B Match the correct form of each word in **bold** in Exercise A with its meaning.

1. _____ answers

2. _____ personal, for just one person

3. _____ to make

4. _____ almost the same

5. _____ worry

6. _____ relationships

7. _____ to think about

8. _____ unknown people

9. _____ ideas

10. _____ all of the people in one group or area

C The words in the box collocate with the noun **connection**. Complete the sentences with the correct words.

build	direct	emotional	with

1. There is a(n) _____ connection between the amount of exercise you do and your health.

2. The police arrested a few people in connection _____ the robbery.

3. Through organizing local events, the city committee is finding ways to _____ stronger connections among people in the community.

4. A great movie is one that allows people to form a(n) _____ connection with the story and its characters.

D Complete the passage using the correct form of the words in **bold** from Exercise A.

Maintaining social ^{1}_____ with people in your ^{2}_____ used to be straightforward. You might have a chat with a ^{3}_____ in your neighborhood, or join a club and get to know people with ^{4}_____ interests to yours. Ever since the 2020 pandemic, more people have started to connect online. A 2021 survey showed that group messaging apps, voice and video calls, and social media were the most common ways people connected with others. However, not everyone may feel comfortable talking about their ^{5}_____ and feelings online, even in ^{6}_____ conversations. Although these communication tools allow immediate ^{7}_____, 68 percent of people who interacted online felt it still wasn't as good as face-to-face communication. And among those who used video calls, 40 percent said they often felt tired from spending time on calls.

COMMUNICATE

E Work with a partner. Discuss the questions below.

1. Which two topics were the responses on the wall most frequently about? Why do you think so many of the responses are about these two topics?

2. How would you complete Candy Chang's sentence on the wall?

Viewing and Note-taking

BEFORE VIEWING

A 🎧 Listen and complete the notes about Candy Chang's "Before I Die" project with the examples for each topic.

1. Travel

   e.g., I want to ride _____ to South America.

   I want to travel _____ with my friends.

2. Family

   e.g., I want to take good care of my _____.

   I want to be a good _____.

> **Note-taking Skill**
>
> **Noting Examples**
>
> Speakers often give examples to support their main ideas. When taking notes, list and indent the examples underneath the topic they describe. You can use the short form "e.g." to mean "for example."

B You are going to watch a class discussion about another project by Candy Chang in which she gets people to share their hopes and anxieties. What kinds of responses do you think Chang received? Note your ideas and discuss them with a partner.

What people are hopeful about	What people are anxious about

WHILE VIEWING

C ▶ **LISTEN FOR EXAMPLES** Watch Segment 1 of the class discussion. Complete the notes with the main ideas and examples for each.

I'm hopeful because …	**Topics:** 1_____ and 2_____
	
	 e.g., 1: … I have a wonderful spouse and great
	             friends who 3_____.
	
	      2: … my mother is becoming more
	          4_____.
	
	      3: … of 5_____.
	
	      4: … of 6_____.

I'm anxious because …	**Topic:** 7_____
	
	 e.g., 1: … people are addicted to 8_____.
	
	      2: … of 9_____.
	
	 Topic: 10_____
	
	 e.g., 1: … 11_____ are dying.
	
	      2: … 12_____ is real and is
	          happening fast.

Listening Skill

Recognizing Examples

Speakers often include examples to illustrate their ideas. Listen for the following phrases to help you identify examples: *for example … , for instance … , such as … , like … , an example of …*

D ▶ **LISTEN FOR DETAILS** Watch Segment 2 of the class discussion. Match each speaker (1–3) to the most suitable description (a–c).

1. Ana   **2.** Mateo   **3.** Mika

_____   _____   _____

a. thinks sharing our feelings can help build human connections.

b. probably would not write a response.

c. believes the project helps people have hope for the future.

AFTER VIEWING

E **APPLY** What do you feel hopeful for and anxious about? Do a class survey. Follow the steps below.

1. On two pieces of paper, complete the sentences "I'm hopeful because …" and "I'm anxious because …". Don't write your name on them.

2. Choose two classmates to collect the papers and group them into those expressing "hope" and those expressing "anxiety." They will then read out the responses from the class.

3. Discuss the results as a class. What are the most common topics?

UNIT 1

Noticing Language

LISTEN FOR LANGUAGE *Agree and disagree*

A Read the expressions below. Write "A" when they are used to agree and "D" when they are used to disagree. Discuss your answers with a partner.

> **Communication Skill**
> **Agreeing and Disagreeing**
> Speakers can use different phrases to show how strongly they agree or disagree with another speaker during a discussion.

1. _____ I disagree.

2. _____ Good point.

3. _____ I don't think so.

4. _____ Absolutely.

5. _____ I'm not sure (about that).

6. _____ Exactly.

7. _____ I agree.

8. _____ I was just about to say that.

9. _____ I don't know.

B 🎧 Listen to the following excerpts from the class discussion in Lesson B. For each statement, choose whether the other speaker agrees or disagrees. Then write the phrase that the speaker used.

1. Mateo: "I think sharing our feelings with someone else makes us feel better."

   Mika **agrees** / **disagrees** using the phrase "_____."

2. Mika: "People reconnect with their values by sharing their feelings about the future."

   Thomas **agrees** / **disagrees** using the phrase "_____."

3. Mateo: "Sharing our feelings with others makes us feel better and builds human connections."

   Ana **agrees** / **disagrees** using the phrase "_____."

4. Mateo: "Sometimes it is easier to share our feelings in public with strangers."

   Thomas **agrees** / **disagrees** using the word "_____."

C Use suitable expressions from Exercise A to complete the responses. Take turns reading your responses aloud to a partner.

1. "Giving a speech in front of many people makes me nervous and anxious."

   _____. I remember the last time when I gave a speech I couldn't sleep well the night before.

2. "Traveling helps take my mind off stressful situations."

   _____. I prefer staying home and reading when I feel stressed.

3. "It's hard to start a conversation with a stranger."

   _____. I find it easier to talk to strangers because I don't have to worry what they might think of me. I won't see them again!

Harvard Square in Massachusetts, U.S.A., is a lively area with shops and restaurants. It's a popular hangout for local residents and students of nearby Harvard University.

D 🎧 Listen to a conversation between two friends. Circle the correct answers.

1. Eric **agrees** / **disagrees** that Janice's neighborhood is a pleasant place to live.

2. Eric **agrees** / **disagrees** with Janice that neighbors have few interactions with one another nowadays.

3. Janice **agrees** / **disagrees** with Eric that she should try to start conversations with her neighbors more often.

COMMUNICATE

E Read the following statements and check (✓) the ones that you agree with. Then tell a partner which statements you agree with and why.

1. ☐ It's easier to share your feelings with someone you don't know very well.

2. ☐ Projects like the one by Candy Chang are a great way to connect people in a community.

3. ☐ I would prefer to have just a few close friends than a big group of friends.

> I agree that it's better to have just a few friends that I'm close to rather than have many friends.

> Really? Why?

> Because these friends are more likely to know me well and support me whenever I need help.

Communicating Ideas

LEARNING OBJECTIVES

- Use appropriate language for agreeing and disagreeing
- Collaborate and explore different ways of connecting with people

> **ASSIGNMENT**
>
> **Task:** You are going to collaborate in a group to discuss different ways of connecting with people.

LISTEN FOR INFORMATION

A 🎧 **LISTEN FOR MAIN IDEAS** Listen to two people discussing whether social media really connects people. Complete the left column of the chart with the reasons they give.

Topic: Social media isn't actually connecting people.		
	Reasons	Examples
Agree	• It is difficult to know if people are 1_____. • We spend less time with people who are 2_____.	• People often share 5_____ online, but nobody knows if they really feel that way. • Friends were occupied with 6_____ during dinner.
Disagree	• Social media gives us a way to express 3_____, which keeps us 4_____.	• Talking about one's problems in person can make some people 7_____. • Sharing one's feelings online may be more comfortable because it is 8_____.

B 🎧 **LISTEN FOR DETAILS** Listen again. Complete the right column of the chart with the examples each speaker gives for their view.

COLLABORATE

C "Spending time alone is more relaxing than interacting with others." Do you agree or disagree with this statement? Write down reasons and examples for your opinion.

_____

_____

_____

D Work in a group. Do the majority of your group members agree or disagree with the statement? Share your reasons and examples and note the most common ideas.

Topic: Spending time alone is more relaxing than interacting with others.		
	Reasons	**Examples**
Agree / Disagree		

E Work with a group that has a different view from your group. Take turns sharing your group's ideas.

> Our group agrees with the statement because when we're alone, we can be ourselves and do whatever we want. We don't have to worry about what other people think. For example ...

Checkpoint

Reflect on what you have learned. Check your progress.

I can ...   understand and use words related to social interaction.

anxiety	**community**	**connections**	**private**	**create**
reflect	**responses**	**similar**	**strangers**	**thoughts**

use collocations with the word *connection*.

watch and understand a class discussion about a community project.

note and organize supporting examples.

recognize examples.

notice language for agreeing and disagreeing.

use language for agreeing and disagreeing.

collaborate and communicate effectively to explore different sides of a topic.

A high school student makes a wish at the Kitano Tenmangu shrine in Kyoto, Japan. Many students visit this shrine to pray for luck and success in their studies.

Building Vocabulary

LEARN KEY WORDS

A 🎧 Listen to and read the conversation between two friends who are discussing the PostSecret Exhibit. What's the exhibition about? Discuss with a partner.

Secret Sharing

A: Do you know about the PostSecret exhibition at the Museum of Us?

B: No, what's that?

A: It's an exhibition displaying a **collection** of postcards with people's **secrets** on them. There are secrets posted **anonymously** from all over the world.

B: What are those secrets like?

A: Some are **shocking**, some are **silly**, and some are deep.

B: I'm not sure I understand why people do that. I don't really mind sharing my secrets with my family and friends, but with a stranger? I don't think so.

A: I felt the same until I read the different secrets people shared on their postcards. Maybe sharing secrets with strangers makes them feel more comfortable because it doesn't matter if the secrets are **spread** around.

B: Fair enough. I see where you're coming from.

A: You know what? I read a secret about how someone would save their voicemails, and it **reminded** me of myself because I take many videos of my family. I see it as a way to **preserve** memories. So, although my dad passed away years ago, the videos I took of him help keep his **spirit alive**.

B: It's interesting that you felt connected with someone you didn't know. I guess shared life experiences can bring people closer.

B Work with a partner. Discuss the questions below.

1. What do you think about sharing secrets with strangers? Do you agree more with Speaker A or B?

2. The photo on the previous page shows a student making a wish at the Kitano Tenmangu shrine in Kyoto, Japan. In Japan, people often write their wishes on wooden blocks called *ema*, and display them in temples and shrines. What other wishing traditions do you know about?

C Match the correct form of each word in **bold** from Exercise A with its meaning.

1. _____ not dead

2. _____ the characteristics of a person

3. _____ something known to only a few people

4. _____ to share information with many people

5. _____ embarrassing; not serious

6. _____ a group of things of the same type

D Complete the sentences using words in **bold** from Exercise A.

1. The news about the young singer's death was _____.

2. This letter was sent to me _____. There isn't a name on it.

3. The local government is working to _____ the beautiful old homes in our community.

4. I'd forgotten about our meeting until Juan _____ me.

E The verbs in the box collocate with the noun **secret**. Complete the sentences using the correct form of the words.

discover	remain	leak	keep	reveal

1. How pyramids were built _____ a secret till this day.

2. A magician never _____ his secrets.

3. She tells everyone everything she hears; you can't expect her to _____ a secret.

4. An employee was disciplined for _____ the company's secrets to the media.

5. After much experimenting, I've _____ the secret to roasting the perfect duck.

COMMUNICATE

F Note your answer to each question below.

1. Who do you often share your secrets with?
   I often share my secrets with my friends.

2. Do you think people should be allowed to comment anonymously on websites?
   I think it is bad thing. because it makes people die.

3. What was the most shocking piece of news you've ever heard?
   That's when I heared the news that we had to wear masks during COVID period

4. What's one way we can preserve our culture and traditions?
   We should know that in detail and show interest.

G Work with a partner. Take turns asking and answering the questions in Exercise F.

> I'm very close with my brother, so I trust him with my secrets. He's reliable and a good listener.

> For me, it's my best friend. I talk to her whenever I have any problems.

Viewing and Note-taking

LEARNING OBJECTIVES

- Watch and understand a talk about a project on sharing secrets
- Notice linking sounds

TEDTALKS

Frank Warren is the creator of the community art project, PostSecret.com, a website for people to share their secrets. He has published five books about the secrets he collected on the website. In his TED Talk, *Half a Million Secrets*, he shares some secrets he collected and explains how sharing secrets can bring people together.

BEFORE VIEWING

A Read the information about Warren's project below. What do you think happened after he handed out the postcards? Discuss with a partner.

> Warren's project began as a small experiment in 2004. He handed out blank postcards to people on the street. Warren asked people to write something on the postcard that they'd never told anyone before and mail the postcards back to him.

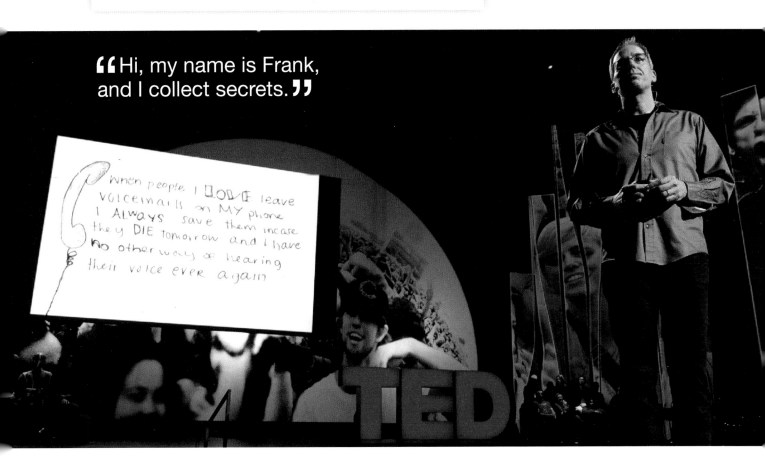

❝Hi, my name is Frank, and I collect secrets.❞

WHILE VIEWING

B ▶ **LISTEN FOR MAIN IDEAS** Watch Frank Warren's TED Talk. Choose the statement that best summarizes his main idea.

    a. Most people prefer to share their secrets with strangers.

    b. Secrets can be powerful in creating shared experiences among people.

    c. Everyone needs to have someone they can share their secrets with.

C ▶ **LISTEN FOR EXAMPLES** Watch the TED Talk again. Complete the notes with the examples Warren gives to support the idea below.

Idea: Secrets can take many forms. They can be shocking, silly, or soulful.

    e.g., 1: "I found these stamps as a child, and I have been _____ to have someone to send them to. I never did have someone."

        2: "I give decaf to people _____ to me."

        3: "Dear Birthmother, I have great parents. _____. I'm happy."

        4: "Inside this envelope is the ripped up remains of a suicide note I didn't use. I feel like _____ on Earth (now)!"

        5: "When people I love leave voicemails on my phone, I _____ in case they die tomorrow and I have no other way of hearing their voice ever again."

D **INFER** Choose the most suitable word or phrase to complete each statement.

1. The person who wrote the postcard about the stamps probably feels _____ now.

    a. anxious   **b.** glad

2. The writer gave the customers decaf coffee because they _____.

    a. were annoyed at them   **b.** made a mistake

3. The sender of the "birthmother" postcard probably _____ their biological mother.

    a. met   **b.** does not know

4. The writer who sent a ripped-up suicide note probably _____.

    a. had a difficult time in the past   **b.** met someone important to them

5. The person who sent the song wanted to _____.

    a. celebrate a birthday   **b.** remember someone

WORDS IN THE TALK

birthmother (n) biological mother of a child who was adopted by other people
decaf (n) coffee that does not contain caffeine
frailty (n) weakness
humanity (n) understanding and kindness toward other people
soulful (adj) full of feeling

AFTER VIEWING

E SUMMARIZE Work with a partner. What kinds of secrets did Warren reveal in his talk? Complete the mind map with the examples of secrets (1–5) from his talk. More than one answer may be possible.

1. The "stamps" secret

2. The "Starbucks" secret

3. The "birthmother" secret

4. The "suicide" secret

5. The "voicemail" secret

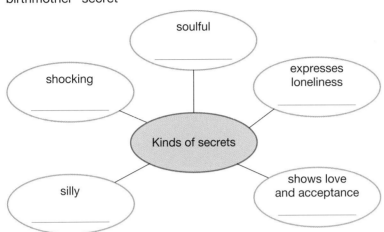

PRONUNCIATION *Linking sounds*

F 🎧 Listen to the excerpts from the TED Talk. Add link marks to the sentences. The first one has been done for you.

1. "And I handed out these postcards randomly on the streets of Washington, D.C., not knowing what to expect."

2. "This one does a great job of demonstrating the creativity that people have when they make and mail me a postcard."

G 🎧 Draw link marks in the excerpts below. Then listen and check your answers.

1. "Inside this envelope is the ripped up remains of a suicide note I didn't use. I feel like the happiest person on Earth now!"

2. "When people I love leave voicemails on my phone, I always save them in case they die tomorrow and I have no other way of hearing their voice ever again."

H Draw link marks in the sentences below. Then take turns reading the sentences aloud to a partner using linking sounds.

1. The competition organizer chose a winner randomly from thousands of entries.

2. The police officer received an award for heroism after she saved a boy's life.

3. There have been countless attempts to solve the problem, but none of them has succeeded so far.

4. After the fire, the remains of the home were just a few burned pieces of furniture.

> **Pronunciation Skill**
> **Linking Sounds**
>
> Speakers often link words to make their speech sound smooth and fluent. For example, we link the final consonant sound of a word to the beginning vowel sound of the next (e.g., *think of = thin-kof*). We also link the final vowel sound of a word to the first vowel sound of the next one (e.g., *they all, you are*).

Thinking Critically

LEARNING OBJECTIVES

- Interpret an infographic about the connection between personal relationships and our health
- Synthesize and evaluate ideas about forming human connection

ANALYZE INFORMATION

A Look at the infographic below. What activities can you think of as examples of the three categories in the infographic? Write two examples for each and discuss your answers with a partner.

Category 1: Strong relationships and networks

e.g., 1: _____

2: _____

Category 2: Community connection

e.g., 1: _____

2: _____

Category 3: Opportunities for social participation

e.g., 1: _____

2: _____

How do our personal relationships affect our health?

Social isolation and loneliness is becoming a public health problem. According to the World Health Organization, in some countries up to one in three older people feel lonely. Family, friends, and communities therefore play an important part in helping us lead healthy lives through:

Source: The Health Foundation (2019)

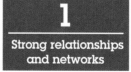

1
Strong relationships and networks

2
Community connection

3
Opportunities for social participation

Strong relationships with family, friends, and colleagues provide emotional support, allow people to develop social skills, and help them face challenges.

Ties within and across communities enable people to help and learn from each other. They also help give people a greater sense of belonging within the community.

Participating in activities within the community offers people a sense of purpose and builds a shared identity. For example, joining a hobby club or volunteering to help local communities.

Volunteers paint a wall in
Los Angeles, U.S.A.

B 🎧 Listen to the podcast and complete the summary below. Write no more than two words for each answer.

A study shows that loneliness may cause physical illnesses like [1]_____ and high blood pressure. To live happier and healthier lives, it's important for us to stay connected with others. We can catch up with our family and friends over a cup of coffee or via a simple [2]_____. We should show our gratitude to our loved ones and remind them of [3]_____ they are to us. We can join a club or take part in [4]_____ to make new friends who share similar interests.

C Think of other ways you can stay connected with your family and friends. Write two examples for each and discuss your ideas with a partner.

	Keep in touch with your family and friends	**Thank your loved ones**
Example 1		
Example 2		

COMMUNICATE *Synthesize and evaluate ideas*

D Compare the ideas from Warren's TED Talk and the infographic and podcast in this lesson. Fill in the blanks with the sources the ideas come from. More than one answer may be possible.

    a. Frank Warren   **b.** the infographic   **c.** the podcast

How we can connect with others

1. share our feelings: _____
2. join a club: _____
3. participate in community activities: _____

Who we should connect with

4. someone we will never meet: _____
5. our family and friends: _____
6. someone with shared interests and identities: _____

E Work with a partner. Discuss the questions below.

1. When is the last time you shared your secrets or talked about your problems with others? How did you feel?
2. Do you think it is necessary for everyone to connect with people in order to be happy? Why, or why not?

Putting It Together

ASSIGNMENT

Group presentation: Your group is going to give a presentation about a
project that can connect people in your community.

PREPARE

A Review the unit. Compare the ideas from the three sources below. What do these
sources encourage people to do?

- Candy Chang's project: A Monument for the Anxious and Hopeful

- Frank Warren's project: The PostSecret Project

- Lesson G infographic: How do our personal relationships affect our health?

B Work with your group. Search online for information about how people in a
community can form closer bonds. Note any useful ideas below.

_____

_____

_____

_____

C Plan your presentation. Work with your group to organize a community project that
can get people together. Use the chart below to include details and examples about
the project.

	Details and examples
What is the purpose of the project? Why is it meaningful?	
What will people do in the project?	
How will people benefit from the project?	

D Look back at the vocabulary, pronunciation, and communication skills you've learned in this unit. What can you use in your presentation? Note any useful language below.

_____

_____

_____

_____

E Below are some ways to begin a presentation. Decide which one works best for your presentation and add that to your plan.

- tell a story
- share a quote or an example
- ask a question
- show an interesting photo

> **Presentation Skill**
>
> **Starting Strong**
>
> A strong start makes the audience think and makes them want to know what comes next. In Frank Warren's TED Talk, he begins by telling a story. Other ways of starting strong are by sharing a quote or interesting example, asking a challenging question, or showing a powerful picture.

F Practice your presentation. Make use of the presentation skill that you've learned.

PRESENT

G Give your presentation to another group. Watch their presentation and evaluate them using the Presentation Scoring Rubrics at the back of the book.

H Discuss your evaluation with the other group. Give feedback on two things they did well and two areas for improvement.

Checkpoint

Reflect on what you have learned. Check your progress.

I can ... understand and use words to talk about secrets.

alive	**anonymously**	**collection**	**preserve**	**remind**
secret	**shocking**	**silly**	**spirit**	**spread**

  use collocations with the word *secret*.

  watch and understand a talk about sharing secrets.

  notice and use linking sounds to make speech smooth and fluent.

  interpret an infographic about how personal relationships affect our health.

  synthesize and evaluate ideas on the importance of human connection.

  give a presentation with a strong start.

  give a presentation about how a community can be better connected.

A grandfather trims a bonsai as his grandson looks on. Bonsai is an art form, and growers work to style their plants into beautiful shapes.

2

Expectations

Q How should we manage people's expectations of us?

Everyone has hopes and dreams, but sometimes we also have to think about other people's dreams about our future, such as our family's. Families may believe that it is important for their children to continue their traditions and practices, or learn a certain skill to have a bright future. Sometimes, however, their expectations may not match ours. In this unit, we'll learn more about how to manage the expectations of other people.

THINK and DISCUSS

1 Look at the photo and read the caption. What kind of expectation(s) do you think the grandfather might have of his grandson?

2 Look at the essential question and the unit introduction. What are some general expectations that people may get from their families?

Building Vocabulary

LEARN KEY WORDS

A 🎧 Listen to and read the information below. Check (✓) the expectations your family have/had of you. Tell a partner about one of them.

Realistic Expectations

Your family may have high **expectations** for your career and personal life. Maybe they want you to attend a top university. Or they hope you will get a great job with a high **salary**. High expectations can encourage people to work hard, but what happens if your application to a top university is **rejected**, or you get a job that doesn't pay very much?

According to research, increasing parental expectations over the past decades is causing an increase in perfectionism among college students. Professor Thomas Curran, the lead researcher, points out that overly high expectations can be damaging to young people's mental health. Young people may use these expectations as a way of measuring their capabilities. So when things don't **work out**, they may feel **disappointed** and **blame** themselves for not being good enough.

The real cause, however, is a **conflict** between expectations and reality. It's therefore important to learn how to **manage** expectations from other people, and to set **realistic** goals. If you have more realistic expectations, you are more likely to meet them, and everyone can feel happy and **proud** instead.

COMMON PARENTAL EXPECTATIONS

- Do well in your studies.
- Go to college.
- Get a good job with a good salary.
- Be independent.
- Help support your family.
- Help out with household chores.
- Follow a particular schedule or routine.

B Match the correct form of each word in **bold** in Exercise A with its meaning.

1. _proud_ feeling pleased about something you have done

2. _realistic_ possible to do

3. _salary_ money you get from your job

4. _disappointed_ unhappy because something was not as expected

5. _expectations_ what you think or hope will happen

6. _manage_ to deal with something effectively

7. _blame_ to think someone is responsible for something bad happening

8. _conflict_ a situation in which things don't fit together

9. _work out_ to happen as planned

10. _rejected_ to not choose or accept something

C The words in the box collocate with the noun **expectations**. Complete the sentences using the most suitable words.

fulfill	manage	exceeded	set

1. The online course that I took didn't really _manage_ my expectations.

2. You can learn to _set_ other people's expectations successfully.

3. It is important to _fulfill_ realistic expectations, not ones that are too high.

4. I didn't think the food would be good but it has _exceeded_ my expectations.

D Complete the passage using the correct form of the words in **bold** from Exercise A.

Should we ¹_set_ parents for having high ²_fulfill_ of their children? In Curran's view, parents may simply be anxious to help their children succeed in an increasingly competitive world. Things like good academic results and jobs with high ³_manage_ are often viewed as indicators of success. Thus, Curran believes that a bigger problem is the amount of pressure that society places on young people. So how can parents help their children deal with expectations and set ⁴_exceeded_ goals? Curran suggests that it's important for parents to teach their children that it's OK even if they fail or if things don't ⁵_set_ as they wanted. Also, instead of focusing on things like test grades, they could pay more attention to their children's learning and personal development.

COMMUNICATE

E Work with a partner. Discuss the questions below.

1. How do you deal with unrealistic expectations people have of you?
2. Can setting high expectations be a good thing sometimes? Why, or why not?

UNIT 2
A B C D

Viewing and Note-taking

LEARNING OBJECTIVES

- Watch a video podcast about managing expectations
- Use a mind map to take notes
- Listen for key ideas by noticing repeated points

BEFORE VIEWING

A 🎧 Listen to someone comparing expectations of women in the past and now. Complete the notes in the mind map.

Note-taking Skill
Using Mind Maps

A mind map is a visual way to organize notes on main ideas and important details. It gives a picture of how ideas are related.

Expectations of women

In the past

Now

Young women expected to ¹ _get married_, ² _have children_, take care of the home.

Few women ³ _against ed_ the expectations by the community.

Education: Young women ⁴ _go to college_.

Work: They ⁵ _get job_ like men.

B You are going to watch a video podcast about managing expectations from one's family. Do you think it's more important to follow your own dreams or meet family expectations? Why? Discuss with a partner.

WHILE VIEWING

C ▶ **LISTEN FOR MAIN IDEAS** Watch Segment 1 of the video podcast. Check (✓) the topics the speaker talks about.

1. ☐ the common types of expectations from one's family

2. ☐ reasons for parents' expectations of their children's career choices

3. ☐ how children can learn to better manage their family's expectations

4. ☐ what children think about their parents' expectations

Listening Skill

Listening for Key Ideas

Speakers usually refer to key ideas several times in a presentation. They may repeat the same word or idea or refer to it in a different way. Listening for key ideas can help you understand what the speaker thinks is important.

D ▶ **LISTEN FOR DETAILS** Watch Segment 2 of the video podcast. Complete the mind map about the experiences of J, W, and M.

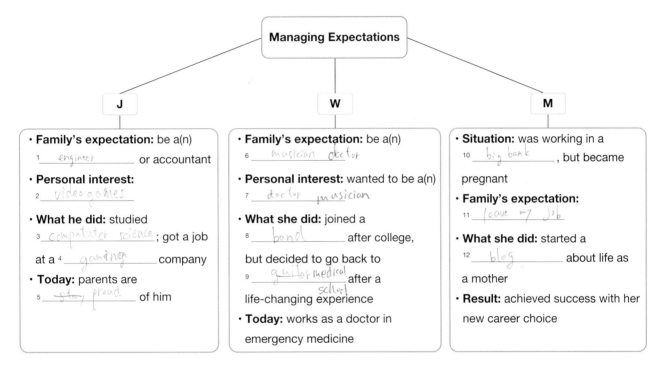

Managing Expectations

J
- **Family's expectation:** be a(n) ¹ _engineer_ or accountant
- **Personal interest:** ² _video games_
- **What he did:** studied ³ _computer science_; got a job at a ⁴ _gaming_ company
- **Today:** parents are ⁵ _so proud_ of him

W
- **Family's expectation:** be a(n) ⁶ _musician doctor_
- **Personal interest:** wanted to be a(n) ⁷ _doctor musician_
- **What she did:** joined a ⁸ _band_ after college, but decided to go back to ⁹ _guitar medical school_ after a life-changing experience
- **Today:** works as a doctor in emergency medicine

M
- **Situation:** was working in a ¹⁰ _big bank_, but became pregnant
- **Family's expectation:** ¹¹ _leave my job_
- **What she did:** started a ¹² _blog_ about life as a mother
- **Result:** achieved success with her new career choice

AFTER VIEWING

E **INFER** Match the speakers (J, W, M) from the video podcast to the statements they are most likely to say.

1. _M_ Maybe I just wasn't strong enough to reject my family's expectations.

2. _J_ I showed my family that it's possible to follow your interests and still have a great career.

3. _W_ Sometimes your dreams in life can change, and that's OK.

F **REFLECT** What do you think about the way J, W, and M managed their family's expectations? What would you do in each situation if you were them? Discuss with a partner.

Noticing Language

LISTEN FOR LANGUAGE *Express opinions*

A Read the phrases below. Which are used to express a strong opinion? Which can you use if you are not sure what you think? Discuss with a partner.

> **Communication Skill**
> **Expressing Opinions**
>
> There are many different expressions you can use to state your opinion. Some expressions are used to show strong opinions, and some are used to show that you are not so sure.

I imagine …	I'm sure …
I think …	I suppose …
I thought …	If you ask me …
I guess …	It seems to me …

B 🎧 Listen to the following excerpts from the video podcast in Lesson B. Write the phrases the speakers use to express their opinions.

1. "Don't get me wrong. _____I think_____ setting realistic expectations can be a good thing."

2. "_____I imagine_____ all of them want their children to be happy and successful."

3. "_____I'm sure_____ this is because they cared about me, but I just didn't want to do either of those things."

4. "_____I guess_____ sometimes you just have to set your own expectations."

5. "_____If you ask me_____, women can be mothers and have careers."

C 🎧 Listen to the speakers' views on the statements below. Take notes on whether they agree or disagree, and their reasons. Then compare your notes with a partner.

1. "If there are no expectations, there will be no *She agree.* disappointments."

_____She agrees._____

_____expectations = unrealistic goals_____

2. "Parents should have a role in deciding their child's career."

_____She agrees_____

_____They have great experience in life and can give_____
_____good advice_____

3. "I would feel bad if I didn't follow my parents' wishes."

_____He disagrees._____

_____it's important to set his own goals in life_____

D 🎧 Listen and complete the conversation.

Yura: Hi, Jacob. What's wrong?

Jacob: I just went to see a doctor because of a bad headache, but I feel like I didn't get a chance to describe my condition fully. The consultation was over in less than five minutes. I'd <u>expected</u> the doctor to ask me more questions.

Yura: ¹ _I think it's important_ that doctors listen more to their patients. You know, I read an <u>article</u> about how male and female doctors communicate, and it said that generally female doctors spend more time seeing their patients.

Jacob: ² _I guess that's true_. I've had both men and women as my family doctor. And generally, I've found my female doctors to be more <u>attentive</u>.

Yura: ³ _I'm not sure about that_. I've seen many male doctors, and they were all quite attentive. But there was a study that showed that female doctors spent more time listening to their patients than male doctors. On average, female doctors listened for three minutes before interrupting their patient. Male doctors, on the other hand, waited for 47 seconds.

Jacob: That's quite a difference. Well, ⁴ _If you ask me_, I'd like my doctor to pay more attention to what I have to say. ⁵ _I'm sure_ it will help them better understand my condition!

E Work with a partner. Read the conversation in Exercise D aloud. Take turns being Yura and Jacob.

COMMUNICATE

F Think of two or more examples of societal expectations and pressure that people often face. Note them below.

> Many people face pressure to …
>
> - earn money to support their family
> - balance work and time with their family
> -
> -

G Work in a group. Take turns sharing your examples. Do they apply to you or someone you know?

Communicating Ideas

ASSIGNMENT

Task: You are going to collaborate in a group to discuss strategies for managing expectations.

LISTEN FOR INFORMATION

A 🎧 **LISTEN FOR MAIN IDEAS** Below are four possible situations involving expectations. Listen and match the speakers to the situations they describe. One situation is not used.

1. _b_ Speaker A   **a.** goes against their parents' expectations.

2. _a_ Speaker B   **b.** shares their parents' expectations but had to change expectations over time.

3. _c_ Speaker C   **c.** doesn't share their parents' expectations but finds a way to manage the situation.

B 🎧 **LISTEN FOR DETAILS** Listen again. Complete the chart with notes on how the expectations were managed.

	Parents' expectations	Expectations of themselves	How expectations were managed
Speaker A			
Speaker B			
Speaker C			

COLLABORATE

C Read the scenario below.

Max recently graduated from college. His major was in music, and he hopes to join an orchestra as a full-time musician. He has gone to a few auditions but hasn't found a position yet. Max's family runs a restaurant. The business was started by his grandparents and is currently managed by his parents. The restaurant is an important part of the family's history, so Max's parents want him and his younger brother to take over the business.

D Work with a group. Discuss a strategy for Max to manage his expectations and his family's expectations. Think of at least two pieces of advice you would give Max. Make notes below.

Max should ...

☐ follow his dream   ☐ follow his parents' wishes   ☐ do something different

Strategy and advice:

E Work with another group. Share the advice your group would give Max and explain the reasons for it.

> I suppose Max could help out with the family business for now because he hasn't found a position yet.

> If you ask me, I think Max should follow his dream because he seems serious about it.

Checkpoint

Reflect on what you have learned. Check your progress.

I can ...   understand and use words related to expectations.

blame	conflict	disappointed	expectation	manage
proud	realistic	reject	salary	work out

use collocations with the word *expectations*.

watch and understand a video podcast about managing expectations.

use a mind map to take notes.

listen for key ideas by noticing repeated points.

notice language for expressing opinions.

express opinions about societal expectations.

collaborate and communicate effectively to discuss managing different expectations.

A girl in her official space suit at the
SpaceIL headquarters in Tel Aviv, Israel.
The organization works to get young people
interested in science and technology.

Building Vocabulary

LEARNING OBJECTIVES

• Use ten words to talk about career expectations
• Use phrases with *living*, *risk*, and *choice*

LEARN KEY WORDS

A 🎧 Listen to and read the passage below. How do you think most people choose a career? Discuss with a partner.

> ### Work to live, or live to work?
>
> You may have heard of the saying, "Do what you love, and you'll never work a day in your life." It means that people should find something they enjoy doing. After all, work makes up a big part of people's lives. But some other people see work simply as a way to **earn a living**—to support themselves and their family.
>
> So is working to live a comfortable life most important? Or is finding something you're interested in better? It ultimately **depends on** what **matters** most to you, and what your **vision** for the future is. For some people, their goals in life are achieved through work. For example, they may choose to take a **risk** and start their own business, or switch to a job in a completely different field. On the other hand, some people may be happy to have a job that pays the bills and allows them time to explore their interests outside of work.
>
> Making career **choices** is not easy, but do something that helps you meet your expectations and goals in life.

B Work with a partner. Think of your career expectations. Discuss the questions below.

1. What does your dream job look like? What do you think the girl in the photo on the previous page dreams of doing?

2. Do you agree with the saying in the passage? Why, or why not?

3. How do you think you would decide on your career?

C Match the correct form of each word in **bold** from Exercise A with its meaning.

1. _depends on_ to be important to someone

2. _earn a living_ to make money

3. _vision_ an idea of how something could be in the future

4. _matters_ a decision between more than one thing

5. _choices_ to be decided by something else

6. _risk_ the possibility that something bad will happen

D Read the excerpts from Hannah Reyes Morales's talk in Lesson F. Choose the options that are closest to the meanings of the words in **bold**.

1. "My job **involves** getting into spaces that other people might not feel comfortable in."

   a. includes   **b.** allows

2. "She thought that photography would **remain** a hobby, a little whimsical activity that I had for myself on the side ... "

   a. develop into   **b.** stay

3. "What would I tell my younger self? I wish I had **trusted** myself more."

   a. believed in   **b.** focused on

4. "I wish I had been more **aware of** what my body was telling me."

   a. alert to   **b.** familiar with

E Below are some common phrases with *living*, *risk*, and *choice*. Complete the sentences using the phrases in the box.

earn a living	reduce the risk of	take a risk	make a choice

1. It was difficult for me to _make a choice_ about my career. I loved languages, math, and music.

2. My father had to start to _earn a living_ at 16 years old after my grandfather passed away.

3. Sometimes it is necessary to _take a risk_ in order to succeed.

4. Frequent exercise and a healthy diet can _reduce the risk of_ diseases and other health issues.

COMMUNICATE

F Think of an example for each item below. Make notes.

1. how you would like to earn a living _____

2. a time when you took a big risk _____

3. someone you trust a lot _____

G Work with a partner. Take turns sharing your ideas in Exercise F.

> I took a big risk when I decided to change my major from Business to Music during my second year in college.

> I think the biggest risk I've taken in my life was moving to another country. I had to learn a new language.

UNIT 2

EF
GH

Viewing and Note-taking

LEARNING OBJECTIVES

- Watch and understand a talk about photography as a career path
- Notice pausing in thought groups

NATIONAL GEOGRAPHIC EXPLORER

NATIONAL GEOGRAPHIC EXPLORER

Hannah Reyes Morales is a National Geographic Explorer. She is a photographer and journalist from the Philippines. Her work focuses on people who live and work in very difficult conditions. In her talk, *Pursuing Your Passion*, she discusses her choice to become a photographer.

BEFORE VIEWING

A Read the information in Hannah Reyes Morales's profile. What skills or personality traits should a photographer have? What kinds of challenges do you think they might face in their job? Discuss with a partner.

❝There were days where I was wondering if I've made the right choice.❞

PART 2 **35**

WHILE VIEWING

B ▶ **LISTEN FOR MAIN IDEAS** Watch Segment 1 of Hannah Reyes Morales's talk. Check (✓) the topics she talks about.

1. ☐ what inspired her to be a photographer
2. ☑ the challenges she had when she started working *wedding*
3. ☐ how she learned photography
4. ☐ how she made her career choice

C ▶ **LISTEN FOR DETAILS** Watch Segment 2 of Reyes Morales's talk. Complete the notes in the chart.

Hannah Reyes Morales's career path	
Advice to her younger self	**Hopes and expectations of her job**
Wished she had ... • trusted herself more • *trusted my own vision and sensibility* Wished she hadn't ... *Tried to throw myself into shapes that I wasn't* *Copied what others were doing*	*not grammars* *lifestyle* *in trusted other people stories* *gratest hounor*

D **LISTEN FOR DETAILS** For each statement below, write **T** (true), **F** (false), or **NG** (not given) if there isn't enough information.

resource

1. __T__ Reyes Morales started taking photos from a young age.

2. __F__ Photography taught Reyes Morales to work well with people.

3. __F__ Reyes Morales's mother supported her career choice.   *hobby*

4. __F__ Reyes Morales's job takes her to dangerous places at times.   *out of her comfort zone.*

5. __T__ Reyes Morales feels that being able to tell other people's stories is the one of the best parts of her job.

WORDS IN THE TALK
honor (v) to show appreciation or respect
perspective (n) a way of thinking about and understanding something
pursue (v) to try to get something
privilege (n) an opportunity to do something special

AFTER VIEWING

E INFER Choose the most suitable phrase to complete each statement.

1. Reyes Morales might agree that _____.

   a. following your dreams is not always easy

   b. you should find a hobby that helps you in your career

   c. you should learn how to set realistic expectations of yourself

2. When Reyes Morales was younger, she might have tried to make her pictures _____.

   a. different and special

   b. look like someone else's

   c. as beautiful as paintings

3. Reyes Morales might think it's important to learn about the stories of _____.

   a. young people

   b. successful photographers

   c. women of color like herself

4. To Reyes Morales, good photos are ones that _____.

   a. help people make their lives better

   b. tell truthful stories of people around the world

   c. show the beauty of people's living environments

F REFLECT Work with a partner. In Reyes Morales's talk, she mentions that her mother wanted her to find a "real job." Do you think being a photographer is a real job? Why, or why not?

PRONUNCIATION   *Thought groups*

G 🎧 Listen to the excerpts from the talk and note the thought groups using slashes (/). The first one has been done for you.

1. Hi, / my name is Hannah Reyes Morales / and I'm a National Geographic photographer / and explorer.
2. I am from the Philippines, which is an archipelago of more than 7,000 islands.
3. I was born and raised in its capital city, which is Manila.
4. I started taking pictures for the news when I was very young.

> **Pronunciation Skill**
> **Thought Groups**
>
> In spoken English, longer sentences are made up of small thought groups or phrases. Each thought group has one focus word. There is a slight pause and drop in pitch at the end of each thought group. Sometimes, thought groups are indicated by commas in writing.

H Mark the thought groups in the sentences below using slashes (/) like in Exercise G. Then take turns reading the sentences aloud to a partner.

1. To me, a good photograph should tell a story that takes us somewhere we haven't been before.
2. When I was younger, a good photograph was an image of a place that I had never been before.
3. Now, a good photograph for me is something that makes me realize I had never looked at the world that way.

Thinking Critically

LEARNING OBJECTIVES

• Interpret an infographic about factors influencing career choices
• Synthesize and evaluate ideas about career expectations

ANALYZE INFORMATION

A Look at the infographic and answer the questions. Discuss your answers with a partner.

1. Which three factors were most important to the students in the survey?

2. What factors do you think would influence your career choice? How similar are they to the ones in the infographic?

3. Do you think your culture influenced your answer to the previous question?

What influences students' career choices?

There are many factors that influence one's choice of career—individual interests and expectations, opportunities the job gives, and the advice of family and friends. All may play a role in career choice, but how strong is each one? That depends partly on cultural and personal factors. For example, in some cultures, the influence of family may be more important; in others, personal interest may be a stronger influence.

A survey by the Student Research Foundation showed that high school seniors are mostly motivated by their own interests and experience, as well as by adults they're close to, when determining a career path.

71% personal interests

36% mother

27% father

26% other life experience

17% high school experience

17% teacher

Source: Student Research Foundation (2016–2017)

B 🎧 Listen to the podcast and complete the summary below with suitable words. Write only one word for each answer.

Melissa Pandika and her father had different ¹_____ about her career ²_____. He wanted her to become a doctor because it is a job with a good ³_____. She wanted to follow her dream to become a ⁴_____. The difference between her own dreams and her father's created a ⁵_____ for her. A psychologist has some advice for people like Pandika—make sure your parents understand that if you choose a different career, it does not mean you are ⁶_____ them.

C Work with a partner. Discuss the questions below.

1. What factors caused Pandika difficulty in making her career choice at first?

2. Do you think she managed to change her father's opinion about her career choice?

COMMUNICATE *Synthesize and evaluate ideas*

D How are Hannah Reyes Morales and Melissa Pandika's career paths similar? In what ways are they different? Complete the chart with information from Lessons F and G.

	Hannah Reyes Morales	Melissa Pandika
Which types of factors have influenced their career choices?		
What did their parents expect them to do for a living?		
What did their parents think they should do with their interests?		
What are their jobs now?		

E Look at the jobs in the box. If your friends wanted to make one of these career choices, what advice would you give them? Discuss with a partner.

athlete   comic artist   stage actor   vet assistant

I don't think there are a lot of job opportunities for athletes in our country. If you ask me, you should think about going overseas if you really want to do sports.

It seems like acting is something you're interested in. But before you decide, I think it's better to find out more about the challenges of the job.

Putting It Together

ASSIGNMENT

Individual presentation: You are going to interview someone and give a presentation on how they managed expectations about their career choice and how they feel about their choices now.

PREPARE

A Review the unit and answer the questions. Discuss with a partner.

1. What are some ways that people might respond to the expectations that others set for them?

2. What are some factors that affect how and why people choose a career?

B Make a list of people that you could interview. They can be your family or people in your community. Make notes on their job and how long they've been working in that job.

_____

_____

_____

C Plan your presentation. Write four interview questions about the areas below. Add any ideas of your own. Then conduct your interview with one of the people you listed in Exercise B and note their responses.

	Question	Notes
Expectations of their parents or community		
Their personal expectations about their career or life		
Any conflicting expectations and how they managed them		
How they feel about their career choice today		
Your idea(s):		

D Look back at the vocabulary, pronunciation, and communication skills you've learned in this unit. What can you use in your presentation? Note any useful language below.

_____

_____

_____

E Look back at your interview notes. Organize your main points using the chart below and note the words or phrases you can use to emphasize these points during your presentation.

Main Ideas	Possible Expressions

> **Presentation Skill**
> **Repetition for Emphasis**
>
> When a word or phrase is spoken several times, it shows what a speaker wants to emphasize and adds a kind of pattern to the speech. In Hannah Reyes Morales's talk, she repeated the phrase "I wish …" many times to emphasize how she felt about her career.

F Practice your presentation. Make use of the presentation skill that you've learned.

PRESENT

G Give your presentation to a partner. Watch their presentation and evaluate them using the Presentation Scoring Rubrics at the back of the book.

H Discuss your evaluation with your partner. Give feedback on two things they did well and two areas for improvement.

Checkpoint

Reflect on what you have learned. Check your progress.

I can ... □ understand and use words to talk about career expectations.

aware of	choice	depend on	earn a living	involve
matter	remain	risk	trust	vision

□ use common phrases with *choice, living,* and *risk*.

□ watch and understand a talk about photography as a career path.

□ identify and use thought groups.

□ interpret an infographic about factors that influence career choices.

□ synthesize and evaluate ideas about career expectations.

□ use repetition to emphasize ideas.

□ give a presentation on how someone managed expectations about their career choice.

Artist He Peiqi adjusts a building in a model city made of stacks of coins and jade stones.

3

Spending Wisely

Q How should public money be spent?

The photo shows a model of Chongqing city, China, created by artist He Peiqi. He designed and built the model city using over 50,000 coins from 11 different currencies—an example of literally building a city using money.

Similarly, governments around the world use public money to build their countries' roads and bridges, as well as to support education, defense, healthcare, and other necessities. But what about things like arts and culture? Should these also be a government responsibility? In this unit, we'll consider how public money should be spent.

THINK and DISCUSS

1 Look at the photo and read the caption. Do you think the money is spent wisely?

2 Look at the essential question and the unit introduction. What do you think is the most important use of the government's money?

Building Vocabulary

LEARN KEY WORDS

A 🎧 Listen to and read the information below. Which do you think is more effective—hard power or soft power? Why? Discuss with a partner.

What Makes a Country Powerful?

In the past, countries used mostly hard **power** to gain **control** of people and places. Hard power includes the use of **military** strength or **economic** pressure. For example, when one country sends its soldiers to another country or stops trade with it, this **demonstrates** hard power.
But there is another type of power that is more frequently used these days—soft power. Soft power means using **attraction** to **influence** people's opinions and behavior. When a country uses soft power, it tries to **promote** a good image of itself to other countries—or other people—to have them think the way it does and to be like it. Countries can do this with music, film, fashion, or other forms of arts and culture. When people all over the world **admire** a country and want to be like it, the country will have a lot of influence—influence that it probably cannot buy or get with **force**.

The World's Top 10 Soft Power Nations 2021

1. Germany ↑2		6. United States ↓1	
2. Japan ↑4		7. France ↓6	
3. United Kingdom 3←		8. China ↓5	
4. Canada ↑7		9. Sweden 9←	
5. Switzerland ↑8		10. Australia ↑13	

Source: Brand Finance Global Soft Power Index 2021

B Match the correct form of each word in **bold** from Exercise A with its meaning.

1. _____ strong physical action

2. _____ help develop

3. _____ like and respect

4. _____ the act of ruling over people or places

5. _____ relating to money and trade

6. _____ to show clearly

7. _____ having to do with the armed forces

8. _____ to affect how someone or something acts

9. _____ the ability to make others do what you want

10. _____ a quality that makes people like you

C Complete the chart below with the correct words. Then complete the sentences using the most suitable words.

Verb	Noun	Adjective
admire		
	attraction	
	influence	
promote		

1. Creating a video of our city might be a good idea to _____ more foreign visitors.

2. Albert Einstein is considered one of the most _____ scientists of all time.

3. I have a lot of _____ for musicians and artists.

4. The government gives money every year for the _____ of programs in art and culture.

D Complete the passage using the correct form of the words in **bold** from Exercise A.

"Country branding" is how a country shapes its image. This concept has become very popular because the image of a country [1]_____ its [2]_____ development and can strengthen its soft [3]_____ in the world. Tourism and exports are two examples of country branding strategies. Some countries use movies and TV dramas to show their culture, history, and natural scenery in an effort to [4]_____ tourism. Other countries rely on exporting products, for example, Germany and its famous cars.

COMMUNICATE

E Work with a partner. Discuss the questions below.

1. What other strategies can you think of that can help promote a country?

2. What country do you want to visit? Why? What attractions are there?

Viewing and Note-taking

LEARNING OBJECTIVES

- Watch a lecture about hard and soft power
- Use a chart to take notes
- Listen for evidence

BEFORE VIEWING

A Read the introduction of a short talk below. What words would you use to label the columns in the chart?

"Many people admire strong leaders who promote the use of force. But not everyone agrees that this is a good form of government. There are advantages and disadvantages to this type of leadership."

> **Note-taking Skill**
> **Using a Chart**
>
> A chart can be a useful way to organize notes when a speaker is discussing two or more clearly separate things.

B 🎧 Listen to the short talk. Use the chart in Exercise A to take notes. Write two ideas in each column.

C You are going to watch a lecture about the use of soft power. What are some examples of soft power? Share your ideas with a partner.

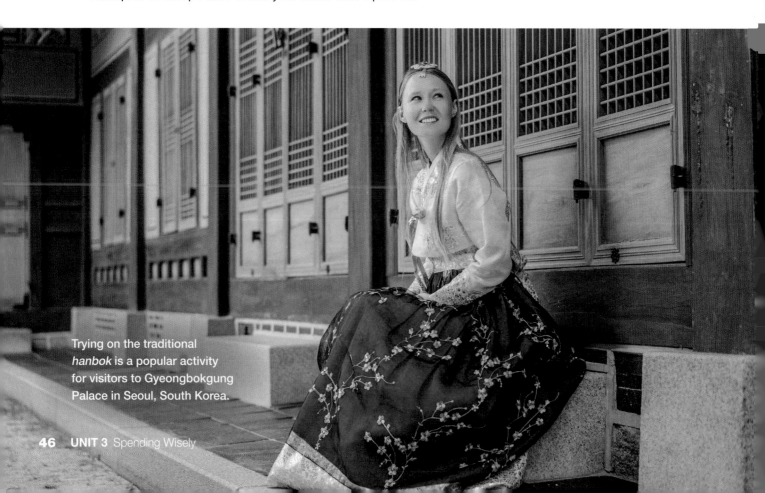

Trying on the traditional *hanbok* is a popular activity for visitors to Gyeongbokgung Palace in Seoul, South Korea.

WHILE VIEWING

D ▶ **LISTEN FOR MAIN IDEAS** Watch Segment 1 of the lecture. What is the main idea?

    a. Hard and soft power are equally important.

    b. Arts and culture can be a very strong form of soft power.

    c. The United States has been a leader in the use of soft power.

E ▶ **LISTEN FOR EVIDENCE** Watch Segment 2 of the lecture. Complete the chart with the evidence the speaker gives to support each idea.

Supporting idea	Evidence
1. Soft power can help the economy.	Findings by the Hyundai Research Institute show that [1]_____ contributes billions of dollars to the [2]_____ every year.
2. More and more people are interested in South Korean culture.	There has been an increase in government-owned Korean [3]_____ around the world.
3. Tourism to South Korea has increased.	A record number of [4]_____ million tourists visited the country in [5]_____.
4. The South Korean government's efforts to increase its country's soft power have been successful.	The country went from [6]_____ place to [7]_____ place in the Portland Soft Power Rankings.

F **LISTEN FOR EVIDENCE** Check (✓) the types of evidence you heard in the lecture.

    a. ☐ a quote by an expert

    b. ☐ statistics

    c. ☐ real-world examples

    d. ☐ research/studies

> **Listening Skill**
>
> **Listening for Evidence**
>
> It is important to support ideas with evidence. Listening for evidence can help you decide if you want to accept a speaker's ideas. Speakers may refer to experts, research, statistics, and real-world examples to support their ideas.

AFTER VIEWING

G **APPLY** Work with a partner. Discuss the statements below.

    1. Describe an example of soft power in your country.

    2. Describe an example of soft power from another country that you think has been successful.

Noticing Language

LISTEN FOR LANGUAGE *Ask follow-up questions*

A The expressions in the box are used to ask follow-up questions. Which can you use for the purposes (1–3) below? Discuss with a partner.

a. Are you saying that …?	**e.** Can you tell me more about …?
b. Do you mean that …?	**f.** I didn't catch that.
c. Did you say …?	**g.** Let me see if I understand.
d. What did you say about …?	**h.** I'm not sure I understand.

1. ask the speaker for more information or to repeat _____

2. say you don't understand something _____

3. ask for a clearer explanation _____

B 🎧 Listen to the following excerpts from the lecture in Lesson B. How did the students ask follow-up questions? Complete the questions below.

1. "_____ arts and culture? Museums?"

2. "_____. Are you saying that the U.S. government planned it like that?"

3. "_____ example? Maybe a more recent one?"

4. "_____ 230?"

> **Communication Skill**
> **Asking Follow-up Questions**
>
> We ask follow-up questions when we are not sure we understand what someone is saying or when we want more information.

C Refer to the questions (1–4) in Exercise B. In which question does the student:

a. ask for more information?

Question _____

b. say they don't understand something?

Question _____

c. ask the speaker to make something clearer?

Questions _____ and _____

D Work with a partner. Take turns explaining the concept of hard and soft power to each other. Use the phrases in Exercise A to ask follow-up questions.

Giant pandas Mei Xiang and Xiao Qi Ji at Smithsonian's National Zoo in the United States.

E 🎧 Listen and complete the conversation with the expressions used to ask follow-up questions.

Professor: So, can anyone give me an example of soft power?

Student 1: Maybe food? Italian food, for example, is very popular and well-known around the world. So, when people think of Italy, they often think of its delicious cuisine.

Professor: That's a great example. What about other types of soft power, such as cultural exchanges between countries?

Student 2: I've read about China's panda diplomacy.

Professor: ¹_____?

Student 2: Well, China sends its giant pandas to some countries to build relationships with them.

Student 1: ²_____ China sends pandas as gifts to other countries?

Student 2: They're actually on loan—and countries have to return them to China after a certain period of time. But yeah, they're kind of like gifts.

Student 1: ³_____. How does this help build soft power?

Student 2: Well, sharing pandas with other countries helps China build friendships. People in other countries also get to learn more about China through this cultural exchange.

Student 1: Oh, that's interesting!

COMMUNICATE

F Choose a topic from the box below or think of one of your own. Make notes about the topic and be prepared to answer questions about it.

your favorite sports team	a famous type of food
your music preferences	a popular TV show

_____

_____

_____

G Work in a group. Take turns to speak for one minute. Ask follow-up questions on other students' explanations.

Communicating Ideas

ASSIGNMENT

Task: You are going to collaborate with a partner to suggest how a country can improve its soft power using arts, culture, food, fashion, sports, or tourism.

LISTEN FOR INFORMATION

A 🎧 **LISTEN FOR MAIN IDEAS** Listen to a talk about France's soft power. Choose the statement that best summarizes the main idea.

    a. France's soft power comes from several sources.

    b. France spends a lot of money to build its soft power.

    c. France topped the soft power rankings for the first time in 2019.

B 🎧 **LISTEN FOR DETAILS** Listen to the talk again. Take notes on the questions below.

    1. What are two reasons for France's high soft power ranking?

        Reason 1: _____

        Reason 2: _____

    2. What evidence does the speaker give of France's popularity with tourists?

        Reason: _____

Mont Saint-Michel, a famous tourist attraction in France

COLLABORATE

C Work with a partner. Think of examples of soft power for the categories below. Note your ideas in the chart.

Area of Soft Power	Country	Example
Arts and culture	*Austria*	*classical music*
Food		
Fashion		
Sports		
Tourism		

D Choose one area of soft power. Think of how a country can promote what they're good at and improve their soft power.

E Share your idea with another pair. The other pair should ask follow-up questions to get more information or check their understanding.

> Austria is known for its classical music. Many famous composers came from there. I think Austria can promote more of its music culture.

> Can you tell me more about ways you think Austria can promote its music culture?

Checkpoint

Reflect on what you have learned. Check your progress.

I can ... understand and use words related to power.

admire	**attraction**	**control**	**demonstrate**	**economic**
force	**influence**	**military**	**power**	**promote**

use noun, verb, and adjective word forms.

watch and understand a lecture about hard and soft power.

use a chart to take notes.

listen for evidence.

notice language for asking follow-up questions.

use expressions for asking follow-up questions.

collaborate and communicate effectively about how countries can improve their soft power.

"The Goddess of Victory" by
Brazilian artist Panmela Castro

Building Vocabulary

LEARN KEY WORDS

A  Listen to and read the conversation below. Do the students agree or disagree with each other? Discuss with a partner.

> **The Importance of the Arts**
>
> **A:** Did you attend the arts festival last week? I don't understand why the school **invests** so much in an event like that.
>
> **B:** I think it was a success. It was an opportunity for many students to demonstrate their **creativity**, and I think events like this are **encouraging**.
>
> **A:** I'm not sure I understand the **value** of the arts. If you ask me, I'd rather the school spend more of its **budget** on new computers or something. At least that would **support** our learning.
>
> **B:** I see what you mean, but I think the arts are an important part of our **society**'s culture. Plus the festival **generated** a lot of interest in our school. I heard that the orchestra's performance at the festival received an **enthusiastic** response.
>
> **A:** Interest in our school? Why is that important?
>
> **B:** The school needs students, right? By holding this kind of event, it can attract new students. From a **financial** point of view, it's worth it.

B Work with a partner. Discuss the questions below.

1. Which student do you agree with? Why?

2. The photo on the previous page shows "The Goddess of Victory," a mural by artist Panmela Castro in Rio de Janeiro, Brazil. It was created for the 2016 Olympics Games. Where can you find or see art in your city?

C Match the correct form of each word in **bold** from Exercise A with its meaning.

1. _____ a sum of money that is available for spending

2. _____ the ability to use imagination and produce new ideas

3. _____ showing a lot of excitement about something

4. _____ importance or significance

5. _____ to create or bring about something

6. _____ giving confidence or hope

7. _____ to help

8. _____ related to money

9. _____ to put money into something that you hope will be worth more later

10. _____ a large group of people living in a certain country or following a particular way of living

D Complete the chart below with the correct words. Then complete the sentences using the most suitable words.

Verb	Noun	Adjective
	creativity	
enthuse		enthusiastic
support		
	value	

1. My family is always _____ of the decisions I make.

2. It is sometimes difficult for _____ people, like artists and musicians, to find jobs.

3. The paintings in the museum are very _____. Some of them are worth millions of dollars.

4. The students showed a lot of _____ for their history projects. I think they really enjoyed themselves.

COMMUNICATE

E Note your answer to each question below.

1. What are you enthusiastic about in arts and culture, e.g., food, fashion, music? What do you like about it?

   _____

2. What's one way of generating greater interest in the arts?

   _____

3. What do you think your school should invest in to better support your learning?

   _____

F Work with a partner. Take turns sharing your answers in Exercise E. Respond to your partner's ideas or ask follow-up questions.

Artist Paul Gauguin's painting "When Will You Marry?" was one of the most expensive artworks ever sold, at around 300 million dollars.

Viewing and Note-taking

LEARNING OBJECTIVES

- Watch and understand a talk about funding for the arts
- Notice the pronunciation of numbers

TEDTALKS

Hadi Eldebek is a musician and educator who develops artistic, cultural, and educational projects around the world. In his TED Talk, *Why Must Artists Be Poor?*, Eldebek discusses his decision to pursue a career in music and also argues that governments should do more to support artists.

BEFORE VIEWING

A ▶ Watch an excerpt from Hadi Eldebek's TED Talk. What do you think will happen to him? Discuss your ideas with a partner.

“Do we think of arts as a luxury or a necessity?”

WHILE VIEWING

B ▶ **LISTEN FOR EVIDENCE** Watch Hadi Eldebek's TED Talk. Complete the chart with the evidence he gives to support each idea.

Idea	Evidence
It is difficult for artists to make a good living.	• Many of Eldebek's artist friends have to take on a(n) 1 _____ . • Only 2 _____ of arts school graduates become professional artists.
Some governments do more than others in supporting the arts.	• Creative Europe (E.U.): 3 _____ billion in funding for over 4 _____ artists • The NEA (U.S.): 5 _____ million in arts funding
The arts industry contributes a lot to a country's economy.	• It generates 6 _____ billion for the U.S. economy. • It supports 7 _____ million jobs. • It pays 8 _____ billion in taxes.

C LISTEN FOR NUMBERS Choose the correct representations of Eldebek's description of arts funding in the United States.

1. Budget for military spending vs. NEA funding for artists

a. Budget for military marching bands = ½ × NEA funding for artists

b. Budget for military marching bands ≈ 2 × NEA funding for artists

2. How a fraction of the military and defense budget could support the arts

a. 0.05% of military and defense budget = (20 orchestras × $20m) + (80,000 artists × $50,000 annual salary)

b. 1% of military and defense budget = (20 orchestras × $20m) + (50,000 artists × $80,000 annual salary)

D ▶ **LISTEN FOR DETAILS** Watch the TED Talk again. For each statement below, write **T** (true), **F** (false), or **NG** (not given) if there isn't enough information.

1. _____ Eldebek's family encouraged him to have a career in music.

2. _____ Eldebek wants people to recognize that the arts have both economic and cultural value.

3. _____ The majority of schools in the U.S. experience budget cuts to arts education programs.

4. _____ Surveys show that most people believe that artists are poor but happy.

WORDS IN THE TALK
angle (n) a position or an opinion
fund (v) to provide money for a purpose
revenue (n) money gained from selling something

AFTER VIEWING

E SUMMARIZE Complete the summary using the correct words in the box.

financial	support	earn a living	society

Problems

- Artists often have to [1]_____ with more than one job.

- The government does not provide enough [2]_____ for artists.

Reasons to support artists

- Artists make an important [3]_____ contribution to the economy.

- The arts bring people together and express ideas that are important in our
  [4]_____.

F INFER Work with a partner. In Eldebek's TED Talk, he says, "Do we think of arts as a luxury or a necessity?" What kinds of attitudes toward the arts does this question show? What would Eldebek's answer to the question be?

PRONUNCIATION *Numbers*

G 🎧 Listen and repeat the numbers and dates below.

1. 60	**6.** 1,002
2. 16	**7.** 2,225
3. 1.5%	**8.** in 2022
4. 0.08	**9.** 5,400,000,000
5. $182	**10.** 235,000,000

> **Pronunciation Skill**
> **Numbers**
>
> Pronouncing numbers correctly helps you to give accurate information. Some numbers or dates can be read in more than one way.

H 🎧 Work with a partner. Take turns reading the sentences below aloud. Then listen and check your pronunciation of the numbers.

1. "The U.S. Census Bureau states that only 10% of art school graduates ... "
2. "Creative Europe will give $2,400,000,000 to over 300,000 artists."
3. "If that's only 0.05%, imagine what a full 1% could do."
4. "It employs 5,700,000 people."

I Work with a partner. Take turns reading the sentences below aloud. Pay attention to the pronunciation of numbers.

1. According to a report, the global arts market had a value of $405.1 billion in 2021.
2. The global arts market is expected to reach $552.6 billion in 2025.
3. The Asia Pacific region made up 31% of the global arts market in 2020.

Thinking Critically

ANALYZE INFORMATION

A   Look at the infographic and answer the questions. Discuss your answers with a partner.

1. Which of these functions is most related to the topic of Eldebek's TED Talk?

2. How does it compare to spending in other categories?

3. Which of these functions is most related to hard power?

4. Based on what you learned in the TED Talk, how do you think spending in the European Union compares to spending on arts and culture in the United States?

5. How do you think this compares to spending on arts and culture in your country?

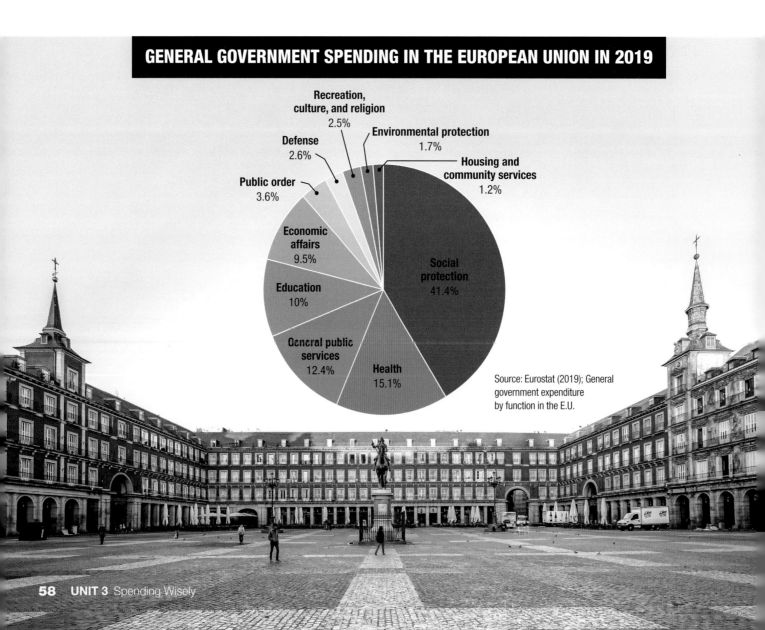

GENERAL GOVERNMENT SPENDING IN THE EUROPEAN UNION IN 2019

Recreation, culture, and religion
2.5%

Defense
2.6%

Environmental protection
1.7%

Public order
3.6%

Housing and community services
1.2%

Economic affairs
9.5%

Social protection
41.4%

Education
10%

General public services
12.4%

Health
15.1%

Source: Eurostat (2019); General government expenditure by function in the E.U.

B 🎧 Listen to the podcast and complete the summary below. Write only one word for each answer.

Sarah Green believes that funding the arts is important because it allows children to experience art and also brings art events to smaller ¹_____.

Most importantly, she believes that arts and culture have ²_____ and ³_____ value in society, and contribute to our national ⁴_____.

C What arts-related events are there in your school or community? Discuss with a partner.

COMMUNICATE   *Synthesize and evaluate ideas*

D Work with a partner. What do Hadi Eldebek and Sarah Green think are the benefits of funding the arts? Complete the Venn diagram using the ideas (a–d).

> **a.** promotes creativity
> **c.** increases children's exposure to art
> **b.** builds social cohesion
> **d.** generates billions of dollars for the economy

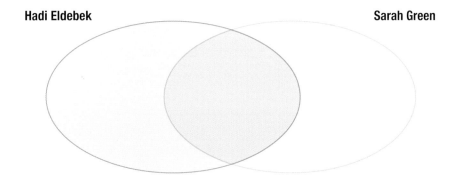

Hadi Eldebek   Sarah Green

E Refer to the ideas in Exercise D. Do you agree with Eldebek and Green? Are there any disadvantages to giving more money to the arts? Discuss with a partner.

Putting It Together

ASSIGNMENT

Individual presentation: You are going to give a presentation on how public money should be spent.

PREPARE

A Review the unit. What does each speaker see as the most important reason(s) for government funding of arts and culture? Make notes in the chart and discuss with a partner.

Speaker	Why should the government support the arts?	Evidence of how arts funding contributes to society?
Lecturer (Lesson B)		
Hadi Eldebek (Lesson F)		
Sarah Green (Lesson G)		

B Search online for how your government spends its money. Make notes on the amount that it spends on the different categories.

_____

_____

_____

_____

C Plan your presentation. Choose two areas that you think your government should spend more money in. Include reasons and evidence to support your ideas.

Area 1	Reasons	Evidence
Area 2	**Reasons**	**Evidence**

D Look back at the vocabulary, pronunciation, and communication skills you've learned in this unit. What can you use in your presentation? Note any useful language below.

_____

_____

_____

_____

_____

E Below are some ways of connecting with the audience. Consider how you can connect with your audience when giving your presentation and add that to your plan.

- tell stories
- use humor
- include pictures
- express your emotions
- share a personal experience
- ask the audience a question

> **Presentation Skill**
> **Connecting with the Audience**
>
> Good presenters try to connect with an audience on a personal level. People are more likely to accept a speaker's message if they feel a connection. In Hadi Eldebek's TED Talk, he connects with his audience by using humor and sharing information about his own life.

F Practice your presentation. Make use of the presentation skill that you've learned.

PRESENT

G Give your presentation to a partner. Watch their presentation and evaluate them using the Presentation Scoring Rubrics at the back of the book.

H Discuss your evaluation with your partner. Give feedback on two things they did well and two areas for improvement.

Checkpoint

Reflect on what you have learned. Check your progress.

I can ... understand and use words related to government spending.

budget	creativity	encouraging	enthusiastic	financial
invest	generate	society	support	value

☐ use noun, verb, and adjective word forms.

☐ watch and understand a talk about funding for the arts.

☐ pronounce numbers and dates correctly.

☐ interpret an infographic about government spending.

☐ synthesize and evaluate ideas on funding for arts and culture.

☐ connect with the audience when giving a presentation.

☐ give a presentation on how public money should be spent.

Armand Duplantis competes in the men's pole vault final during the 2020 World Athletics Indoor Tour in Lievin, France.

4

Aim Lower, Reach Higher?

 How should we set realistic life goals?

Everyone makes plans to achieve their goals. Athletes such as Armand Duplantis (pictured at the 2020 World Athletics Indoor Tour), for example, train hard to be the best at their sport. An Olympic champion, Duplantis has broken several world records and aims to continue setting new records in pole vaulting.

What about other goals that we may have in life, such as our career, studies, or health? How can we set ourselves up for success? In this unit, we'll look at different advice and suggestions on how to set achievable goals.

THINK and DISCUSS

1 Look at the photo and read the caption. What is this person trying to achieve?

2 Look at the essential question and the unit introduction. What are some of your personal goals in life?

Building Vocabulary

LEARN KEY WORDS

A 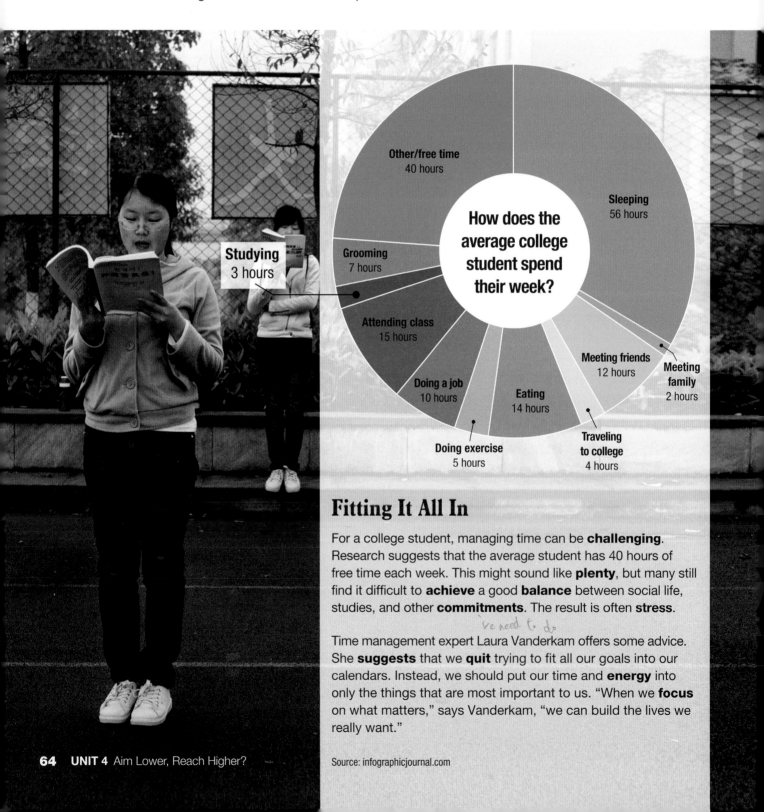 Listen to and read the information below. How similar or different is your week to that of the average student? Discuss with a partner.

Other/free time
40 hours

Sleeping
56 hours

Studying
3 hours

Grooming
7 hours

How does the average college student spend their week?

Attending class
15 hours

Meeting friends
12 hours

Meeting family
2 hours

Doing a job
10 hours

Eating
14 hours

Doing exercise
5 hours

Traveling to college
4 hours

Fitting It All In

For a college student, managing time can be **challenging**. Research suggests that the average student has 40 hours of free time each week. This might sound like **plenty**, but many still find it difficult to **achieve** a good **balance** between social life, studies, and other **commitments**. The result is often **stress**.

Time management expert Laura Vanderkam offers some advice. She **suggests** that we **quit** trying to fit all our goals into our calendars. Instead, we should put our time and **energy** into only the things that are most important to us. "When we **focus** on what matters," says Vanderkam, "we can build the lives we really want."

Source: infographicjournal.com

B Match the correct form of each word in **bold** in Exercise A with its meaning.

1. _suggests_ to mention or introduce an idea
2. _challenging_ hard, difficult
3. _commitments_ things you agreed to do
4. _energy_ strength, power
5. _focus_ to give your attention to something

6. _stress_ pressure, worry
7. _acheive_ to succeed, to reach
8. _balance_ the state of having not too much or too little
9. _quit_ to stop
10. _plenty_ more than enough

C The words in the box collocate with the noun **balance**. Complete the sentences with the correct answers.

achieve	proper	lose	work-life

1. It's dangerous to run near the pool. You might _lose_ your balance and fall in.
2. My ideal job allows me to have a good _proper_ balance.
3. Creating a study schedule is one way to _achieve_ a balance between schoolwork and other activities.
4. A healthy lifestyle requires having a _work life_ balance of diet, exercise, and rest.

D Complete the passage using the correct form of the words in **bold** from Exercise A.

Feeling tired from your studies? Working too hard? ¹_Proper_ a healthy work-life ²_acheive_ in today's busy world can be ³_lose_, and we all need to make time for ourselves. Try the 5-4-3-2-1 method. You need just a few minutes a day. The first step is to manage your breathing: Sit quietly and take some slow, deep breaths. Let your mind relax. Then ⁴_work-life_ on the world around you. Use all your senses to notice:

5	**4**	**3**	**2**	**1**
things you can SEE	things you can FEEL	things you can HEAR	things you can SMELL	thing you can TASTE

This technique helps move your attention away from things that are causing you ⁵_work-life_. That way, you'll have more ⁶_achieve_ for the day ahead.

COMMUNICATE

E Work with a partner. Discuss the questions below.

1. Try the 5-4-3-2-1 method. How did the exercise make you feel? Do you think the exercise could be useful?
2. Do you find it challenging to manage your time? What aspects of time management cause you stress?

Viewing and Note-taking

LEARNING OBJECTIVES

- Watch a webinar about curating your life
- Use symbols for taking notes
- Make predictions about content

BEFORE VIEWING

A Look at the symbols in the box below. Which ones do you usually use? What other symbols do you use? Discuss with a partner.

Symbols

↑	increase, more	∵	because, so
↓	decrease, less	∴	therefore, as a result
→	leads to, results in	>	more than
=	means, is equal to	<	less than
&	and, also	~	about

> **Note-taking Skill**
> **Using Symbols**
>
> Using symbols can improve your note-taking speed and help make sure you don't miss any important information. There are many standard symbols you can use, but you can also develop your own system.

B 🎧 Listen to five sentences. Take notes using symbols and abbreviations. Compare your notes with a partner.

1. The number of students tran   univers
   # of stud @ U ↑ ∵ tuit ↓

2. People esp   have longer working   stressful
   ppl in cities = longer work days → hlth iss
   = jnson

3. is very impor   tri fam ho

4. _____

5. _____

C You are going to watch a webinar about curating your life. Read the definition below. What do you think it means to "curate your life"? Discuss with a partner.

> *curate* (v)   to select and organize the items in a collection, for example in a museum

> **Listening Skill**
> **Make Predictions**
>
> Predicting what you are going to hear can help you follow the ideas more easily. Think about these questions: What type of listening is it? Who's the speaker? What do I know about the topic?

WHILE VIEWING

D ▶ **LISTEN FOR MAIN IDEAS** Watch Segment 1 of the webinar. Take notes using the outline below.

Topic: Managing expectations at uni.

Be a curator = [1]_____

1. Make list of main [2]_____ & [3]_____

    e.g., [4]_____

2. Prioritize. i.e., [5]_____

    Put activities into a [6]_____

    Think about 2 things: [7]_____ & [8]_____

E **PREDICT** Look at the chart and read the sentences (a–d). Predict which box each sentence might refer to and note them in each section of the chart. Discuss your ideas with a partner.

  a. Focus your energy on these activities.

  b. It may be a good idea to drop these activities.

  c. Consider asking for help with these activities.

  d. Be prepared to be just "good enough" at these activities.

	Makes me happy	Doesn't make me happy
Highly important		
Not so important		

F ▶ **LISTEN FOR DETAILS** Watch Segment 2 of the webinar. Check your predictions in Exercise E. Add any examples the advisor mentions in each section of the chart.

AFTER VIEWING

G **APPLY** Read the scenarios below. What advice would you give to each person? Discuss with a partner.

Ayako: I visit my grandparents every Sunday. I love them, but I'd rather spend my time with friends. It makes my mom happy, though. What's your advice?

Raul: Playing in my band is the most important thing in my life. But my parents are always telling me to focus on my studies. What should I do?

Noticing Language

LISTEN FOR LANGUAGE *Make recommendations*

A Read the phrases below. Which phrases do you think are usually used to make stronger recommendations? Which are for less direct recommendations? Discuss with a partner.

a. How about ...	**f.** Why don't we ...
b. It's important to ...	**g.** We should ...
c. It's probably a good idea to ...	**h.** You could consider ...
d. I suggest (that) ...	**i.** You have to ...
e. Think about ...	**j.** You must ...

Stronger recommendations: _____

Less direct recommendations: _____

B 🎧 Listen to the following excerpts from the webinar in Lesson B. Complete the sentences below with the phrases the speaker used for making recommendations.

1. "_____ you start by making a list."

2. "_____ prioritize."

3. "_____ drop them."

4. "_____ joining a reading group."

5. "_____ how you might curate your life."

> **Communication Skill**
> **Making Recommendations**
>
> When making recommendations, it's important to consider carefully the language you use. Some phrases can be used to make strong recommendations while others are less direct.

C Use suitable expressions from Exercise A to complete the recommendations. Read your recommendations to a partner.

1. _____ form good habits and keep them.

2. _____ focus on what really matters.

3. _____ listing out everything we need?

4. _____ going jogging twice a week?

5. _____ manage your energy levels.

6. _____ reducing the amount of time spent on your social commitments.

D Look at the conversations below. For each situation, what recommendation might speaker B give? Discuss with a partner. Think of three possibilities for each situation.

1. **A:** I don't have time for a hobby. I have too much work to do.

   B: I suggest _____.

2. **A:** I have 12 exams in two weeks! How can I organize my study time?

   B: Well, it's really important to _____.

3. **A:** I have too many classes at the moment. I can't decide which one to drop.

   B: You could consider _____.

E  Listen to the conversations. Complete the recommendations. Were any similar to your ideas?

COMMUNICATE

F Choose a topic from the box below. Think of three recommendations and make notes.

How to choose a new phone	How to study for exams	How to remember new words
How to sing better	How to get in shape	How to save money

Topic: _____

1. _____

2. _____

3. _____

G Work in a group. Take turns speaking for one minute. Explain your topic and make your recommendations using the phrases in Exercise A. Add extra details.

> Here are three recommendations for how to save money. First, you might want to think about what you spend most on ...

Communicating Ideas

ASSIGNMENT

Task: You are going to collaborate with a partner to learn about a person and advise on how they might "curate" their life.

LISTEN FOR INFORMATION

A 🎧 **LISTEN FOR MAIN IDEAS** Listen to a conversation between two students, Sofia and Paulo. Check (✓) the statements that are true about Sofia.

1. ☐ Her major is Music. She also studies Business.

2. ☐ She plays the violin and takes lessons, but she doesn't enjoy it.

3. ☐ She has a pet dog and volunteers at a rescue center.

4. ☐ She wants to quit her basketball team.

5. ☐ She wants to look for a part-time job.

6. ☐ She doesn't enjoy socializing and rarely hangs out with her friends.

B 🎧 **LISTEN FOR DETAILS** How does Sofia feel about the commitments and activities in Exercise A? Listen again and complete the outline below.

Studies

Likes/Doesn't like: _____

Important/Not important: _____

Other details: _____

Hobbies

Likes/Doesn't like: _____

Important/Not important: _____

Other details: _____

Other Commitments

Likes/Doesn't like: _____

Important/Not important: _____

Other details: _____

COLLABORATE

C Work with a partner. Use your notes from Exercise B to complete the chart below.

	Makes Sofia happy	**Doesn't make Sofia happy**
Highly important		
Not so important		

D Think of some recommendations you would make to Sofia about how she can "curate" her life. Note them below.

_____

_____

_____

E Share your recommendations with another pair. Explain the reasons for your ideas.

> I think Sofia should quit the basketball team. Although she enjoys it, there are other things that are more important to her, such as spending time with her friends.

Checkpoint

Reflect on what you have learned. Check your progress.

I can ...   understand and use words related to life goals.

achieve	balance	challenging	commitment	energy
focus	plenty	quit	stress	suggest

use collocations with *balance*.

watch and understand a webinar about curating your life.

use symbols for taking notes.

predict content before listening.

notice language for making recommendations.

use language for making recommendations.

collaborate and communicate effectively to give recommendations.

The TCS New York City Marathon is one of the biggest marathon events in the world. It attracts tens of thousands of runners every year.

Building Vocabulary

LEARN KEY WORDS

A  Listen to and read the passage below. What new habit did Christine Carter try to start? Was she successful? Discuss with a partner.

> **Planning for Success?**
>
> During the 2020 global pandemic, writer and sociologist Christine Carter tried to stay positive. "Embrace not being so busy," she wrote in an advice article. "Take this time at home to **get into** a new happiness habit."
> *(join)*
>
> Carter decided to use her time to achieve a big goal: she would train to run a half-marathon. In the first week she carefully planned a training **routine**. The next few weeks went well, but then Carter started to lose **motivation** and ended up missing training runs. In the end, despite all her **effort** in preparing for her run, her **ambitious** plan ended in failure.
> *(unrealistic)*
>
> "Truth be told," says Carter, "for the first few months of the pandemic, I [didn't] follow my own best advice." So, Carter asked herself a question: Why is it often a **struggle** to follow our own plans?

B Work with a partner. Discuss the questions below.

1. Have you ever tried to start a new habit? What was it?

2. How successful were you at starting your new habit?

3. The photo on the previous page shows participants of the 2021 TCS New York City Marathon crossing the Verrazzano-Narrows Bridge. Marathon runners often have to train for months before a race. What kinds of challenges do you think they face while preparing for a marathon?

C Match the correct form of each word in **bold** in Exercise A with its meaning.

1. _____struggle_____ to become interested in

2. _____routine_____ things you do regularly or every day

3. _____get into_____ something that is difficult to do

4. _____effort_____ aiming for great results

5. _____motivation_____ the energy used to do something

6. _____ambitious_____ a feeling of wanting to do something

D Read the excerpts from Christine Carter's TED Talk in Lesson F. Choose the options that are closest to the meanings of the words in **bold**.

1. "To **establish** an exercise routine, … I needed to stop trying to be an actual athlete."

a. start or create *(circled)*   **b.** enjoy very much

2. "New **behaviors** tend to require a lot of effort, because change is really hard."

a. activities we enjoy   **b.** things we usually do *(circled)*

3. "I like being good at things, and I quit exercising because I wasn't **willing** to be bad at it."

a. happy to *(circled)*   **b.** expecting

4. "I started feeling a real **desire** to keep on running."

a. help with doing something difficult   **b.** a feeling of wanting something to happen *(circled)*

E Complete the chart below with the correct words. *Word Hippo Slide go to google*

Noun	Verb	Adjective
ambition	–	ambitious
motivation	motivate	motivational
struggle	struggle	struggling

COMMUNICATE

F Note an example next to each prompt below. Use just a few words.

1. something that is a struggle for you to do _____

2. a routine you follow every day _____

3. a new behavior that you would like to establish _____

4. an ambitious goal you have in life _____

5. your motivation for learning a foreign language _____

G Work with a partner. Cover the prompts and look at your examples. Try to remember why you wrote each one and explain to your partner. Add extra details and ask follow-up questions.

Waking up early in the morning is a real struggle for me.

Why's that?

Viewing and Note-taking

LEARNING OBJECTIVES

- Watch and understand a talk about how to start a new habit
- Notice the use of syllable stress

TEDTALKS

Sociologist **Christine Carter** is the author of *The Sweet Spot: How to Accomplish More by Doing Less*. In her TED Talk, *The 1-Minute Secret to Forming a New Habit*, she shares a simple step to help keep you on track to achieving your goals.

BEFORE VIEWING

A Think about what you learned about Carter in the previous lesson. Predict what you think her 1-minute secret might be. Discuss with a partner.

❝ Take only one step, but take that step every day. **❞**

WHILE VIEWING

B ▶ **LISTEN FOR MAIN IDEAS** Watch Segment 1 of Christine Carter's TED Talk. Choose the correct answer for each question.

1. What does Carter say about motivation?

    a. We can't easily control our level of motivation.

    b. We won't be motivated if our goals aren't ambitious enough.

    c. Celebrating our successes can help increase our motivation level.

2. How does Carter keep herself motivated?

    a. She rewards herself when she meets her goal.

    b. She runs with friends instead of running alone.

    c. She makes sure to complete one easy goal every day.

C ▶ **LISTEN FOR DETAILS** Watch Segment 2 of Carter's TED Talk. For each statement below, write **T** for true or **F** for false.

1. _T_ According to Carter, we can form a habit by starting with something very simple.

2. _T_ In Carter's view, we should try doing something even if we are bad at it.

3. _F_ Carter started running longer because she felt like she needed more exercise.

4. _F_ Carter suggests making our goals more challenging after we achieve the easier ones.

5. _F_ Thanks to her new routine, Carter is now able to run half-marathons.

D **SEQUENCE EVENTS** How did Carter form a new habit? Order the events below (1–6).

a. _____ Carter decides to run a half marathon.

b. _____ Carter starts to feel a desire to keep running.

c. _____ Carter creates a detailed training schedule.

d. _____ Carter decides to run for only one minute at a time.

e. _____ Carter starts skipping training runs.

f. _____ Carter becomes a runner.

WORDS IN THE TALK
audacious (adj) showing a desire to take risks
autopilot (n) the state of doing something without thinking about it
mediocre (adj) average, not good or bad
miniscule (adj) tiny, very small

AFTER VIEWING

E **SUMMARIZE** Complete the diagram using the words in the box to summarize Carter's advice about how to start a new habit.

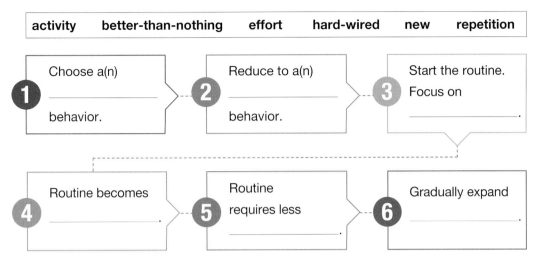

| activity | better-than-nothing | effort | hard-wired | new | repetition |

1 Choose a(n) _____ behavior.

2 Reduce to a(n) _____ behavior.

3 Start the routine. Focus on _____.

4 Routine becomes _____.

5 Routine requires less _____.

6 Gradually expand _____.

PRONUNCIATION *Syllables and stress*

F 🎧 Listen to the excerpts from the TED Talk and notice how Carter pronounces the adverbs below. Write them in the correct place in the chart. Take turns reading each adverb aloud with a partner.

1. optimistically
2. totally
3. incredibly
4. fortunately
5. organically
6. truly

> **Pronunciation Skill**
> **Syllables and Stress**
>
> A syllable contains one vowel sound. In words with more than one syllable, only one of the syllables is stressed. Stressing the correct syllable will help a speaker be clearly understood.

Oo	Ooo	Oooo	oOoo	oOooo	ooOooo
					optimistically

G Complete the sentences using the most suitable words. Then read your sentences aloud to a partner.

| truly | incredibly | totally | definitely |

1. I find changing my habits _____ difficult.

2. I'm _____ going to start a new hobby this year.

3. I have a bad habit that I think is _____ impossible to change.

4. I've thought hard about what I _____ want in life.

H Work with a partner. Discuss which sentences are true for you. Explain why or why not.

Thinking Critically

ANALYZE INFORMATION

A Look at the infographic below and answer the questions. Discuss your ideas with a partner.

1. Look at the top five resolutions. What are they basically about?

_____ and _____

2. Which of the resolutions do you think would be the easiest—and the hardest—for people to keep for a long period? Why?

Easiest: _____

Why? _____

Hardest: _____

Why? _____

> I think saving money as a student is incredibly difficult, especially if you have a lot of living costs like housing.

A New Year – A New Me!

Many people make new life goals, or resolutions, at New Year's—but in most cases, we fail to keep to our plans. Here are the most common resolutions, and how long they are likely to last.

Success rates for resolutions start to drop after two weeks; by the halfway point in the year, more than 50% of people have given up.

THE MOST POPULAR RESOLUTIONS

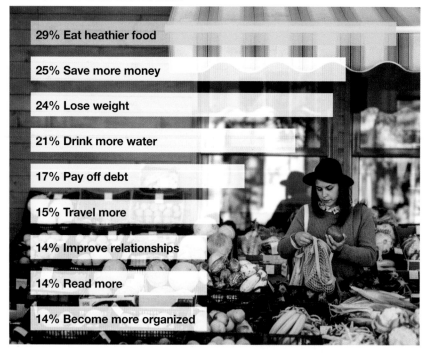

29% Eat heathier food

25% Save more money

24% Lose weight

21% Drink more water

17% Pay off debt

15% Travel more

14% Improve relationships

14% Read more

14% Become more organized

PERCENTAGE OF PEOPLE KEEPING TO THEIR RESOLUTION

75%
Past the first week

71%
Past two weeks

64%
After one month

46%
After six months

Source: The Harris Poll Data refers to % of people interviewed who set this resolution in January 2017.

Source: Journal of Clinical Psychology

B  Read the statements below. Then listen to a talk about Reggie Rivers's ideas for goal-setting. Check (✓) two statements that best summarize the talk.

a. ☐ We worry about our resolutions too much.

b. ☑ We should focus on our behaviors to help achieve our goals.

c. ☑ More than 50% of people give up on their resolutions after six months.

d. ☑ Our to-do lists should be planned in the short term to keep ourselves motivated.

e. ☐ Learning a language is one example of a New Year's resolution.

C Think of something in your life you would like to change or improve. What are some things you could do (1) today, (2) tomorrow, and (3) this week, to help achieve that goal? Discuss your ideas with a partner.

Reggie Rivers

COMMUNICATE   *Synthesize and evaluate ideas*

D Work with a partner. How do Reggie Rivers's ideas compare with Christine Carter's? Complete the Venn diagram.

Christine Carter

Reggie Rivers

E Look at the opinions about Carter's and Rivers's ideas in the chart below. Do you agree with the opinions? Check (✓) your responses and discuss your reasons with a partner.

	Agree	Disagree	Not sure
1. I think Carter's goal of one minute is too short. It's more realistic to aim for five minutes a day if you want to improve.			
2. I like Rivers's idea of focusing on things I can do today and tomorrow. It keeps me motivated especially if I have a long-term goal.			
3. I think we should focus on big, ambitious goals. If we only focus on small changes, we'll only achieve small goals!			

UNIT
4

E F
G H

Putting It Together

ASSIGNMENT

Individual presentation: You are going to give a presentation about three recommendations to answer the question "How can we set life goals that are realistic?"

PREPARE

A Review the unit. How would each of the experts below answer the question "How can we set life goals that are realistic?" Discuss with a partner.

> Dr. Gail Golden (Lesson B)   Christine Carter (Lesson F)   Reggie Rivers (Lesson G)

B Search online for other expert opinions on setting life goals. Note any useful ideas below.

_____

_____

_____

_____

C Plan your presentation. First, decide what you think are the three best recommendations. You can use advice from any of the people above or your own ideas. Include details and examples to make the advice clear. Make notes in the chart below.

Topic: How should we set realistic life goals?		
Recommendation	**Source/Expert**	**Details & Examples**
1.		
2.		
3.		

D Look back at the vocabulary, pronunciation, and communication skills you've learned in this unit. What can you use in your presentation? Note any useful language below.

_____

_____

_____

_____

_____

E Below are some adverbs we can use to add emphasis. Look back at your notes and identify the points you want to emphasize. Think of suitable adverbs you can use with those points and add them to your plan.

- really
- clearly
- simply
- absolutely
- definitely
- extremely

F Practice your presentation. Make use of the presentation skill that you've learned.

PRESENT

G Give your presentation to a partner. Watch their presentation and evaluate them using the Presentation Scoring Rubrics at the back of the book.

H Discuss your evaluation with your partner. Give feedback on two things they did well and two areas for improvement.

Checkpoint

Reflect on what you have learned. Check your progress.

I can ... ☐ understand and use words related to habits.

ambitious	**behaviors**	**desire**	**effort**	**establish**
get into	**motivation**	**routine**	**struggle**	**willing**

☐ use noun, verb, and adjective word forms.

☐ watch and understand a talk about how to start a new habit.

☐ notice syllable stress patterns.

☐ interpret an infographic about New Year's resolutions.

☐ synthesize and evaluate ideas about setting life goals.

☐ use adverbs to emphasize key points.

☐ give a presentation on ways to set realistic life goals.

A local resident stands in flood water in front of her home in Java, Indonesia.

5

Global Countdown

Q How should we respond to environmental problems?

Across the globe, more and more places are seeing the effects of climate change. The island of Java in Indonesia, for example, is experiencing floods more often due to rapidly rising sea levels. In this unit, we'll look at how different countries and communities are responding to environmental issues.

THINK and DISCUSS

1 Look at the photo and read the caption. How does the environmental problem shown in the photo affect people?

2 Look at the essential question and the unit introduction. What environmental problems do you know of? Which are you most concerned about? Why?

Building Vocabulary

LEARN KEY WORDS

A 🎧 Listen to and read the information below. What are some of the effects of climate change in different parts of the world? Discuss with a partner.

Not Just Higher Temperatures

2020 was one of the hottest years ever recorded—both Europe and Asia had annual temperatures that were more than 2°C above average. As a result of climate change, global temperatures are **rising** and our planet is getting hotter. Not all the **effects** of climate change, however, will be felt the same way everywhere. One of the biggest differences will be in the amount of rainfall different places receive. Experts **predict** that in some parts of the world, there will be much less rain in the future, and people there are more likely to **suffer** water shortages. In other parts of the world, there will be a lot more rain, causing **floods**. In Rwanda, for example, the heavy rains in March 2018 led to serious floods, affecting nearly 25,000 people.

To **protect** people and the environment, some countries have taken steps like increasing the use of clean energy and encouraging recycling. While scientists have different views on the amount of time we have left to avoid the worst effects of climate change, most agree that we should step up our **current** efforts to slow down climate change.

Sources: Climate Central; NOAA NCEI 2020 Annual Global Climate Report

10 Hottest Global Years on Record

Difference from average temperature

+1.4°C
+1.0°C
+0.6°C
+0.2°C

2013 2010 2014 2018 2021 2015 2017 2019 2020 2016

B Match the correct form of each word in **bold** in Exercise A with its meaning.

1. _Suffer_ to experience pain

2. _effects_ the result of something

3. _protect_ to keep someone or something safe

4. _rising_ to increase

5. _predict_ to say something will happen before it happens

6. _current_ existing now

7. _floods_ a large amount of water that fills an area that is usually dry

C Read the sentences. Choose the options that are closest to the meaning of the words in **bold**.

1. The project **requires** a lot of energy and hard work.
   a. needs
   b. creates

2. If you leave ice cream in the sun, it will **melt**.
   a. taste bad
   b. become liquid

3. I believe that **ordinary** people, not just government leaders, can slow climate change.
   a. educated
   b. regular

D Complete the chart below with the correct words. Then complete the sentences using the most suitable words.

Verb	Noun
	flood
predict	
protect	
require	
rise	

1. Recycling of plastic should be a _____ in every community.

2. Our homes will need more _____ from storms and forest fires.

3. If it continues raining tomorrow, the whole city will _____.

E Complete the passage using the correct form of the words in **bold** from Exercises A and C.

As global temperatures continue to [1]_____, the [2]_____ of climate change can be seen in an increase in the frequency of natural disasters around the world. In the United States, [3]_____ are one of the most common natural disasters. And scientists [4]_____ that there will be an up to 29% increase in flood risk by 2050. To [5]_____ the areas that are at high risk, the government will need to spend a lot of money to make changes in urban infrastructure.

COMMUNICATE

F Work with a partner. Discuss the questions below.

1. What natural disasters do you think cause the most damage?

2. Do you think that enough is done to protect against natural disasters?

Viewing and Note-taking

LEARNING OBJECTIVES

- Watch a presentation about the impact of global warming on one country
- Use a timeline to take notes
- Listen for time signals

BEFORE VIEWING

A 🎧 Listen to a short talk about the impact of global warming on sea ice. Complete the timeline with the correct information.

Note-taking Skill

Making a Timeline

Speakers sometimes describe a series of events in order of when they happened. Organizing your notes in a timeline can help you follow the sequence of events more easily.

Amount of sea ice

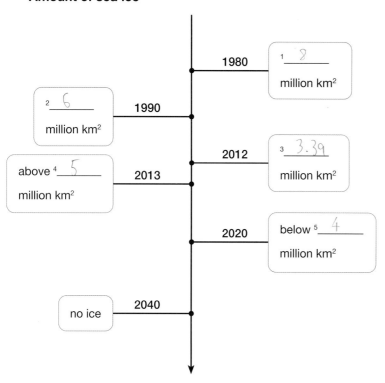

1980 — 1 _8_ million km²

1990 — 2 _6_ million km²

above 4 _5_ million km² — 2013

2012 — 3 _3.39_ million km²

2020 — below 5 _4_ million km²

no ice — 2040

B You are going to watch a presentation about the impact of climate change on the Maldives. What do you know about the Maldives? What effects of climate change do you think the country is experiencing? Discuss with a partner.

WHILE VIEWING

C ▶ **LISTEN FOR MAIN IDEAS** Watch Segment 1 of the presentation. Check (✓) the topics that the speaker talks about.

1. ☐ how climate change is affecting countries around the world

2. ☐ why the Maldives is in danger from the effects of climate change

3. ☐ the steps the Maldives has taken to protect itself

4. ☐ how the country is using technology to find solutions

D ▶ **LISTEN FOR DETAILS** Watch Segment 1 of the presentation again. Complete the timeline to show the steps that the government took.

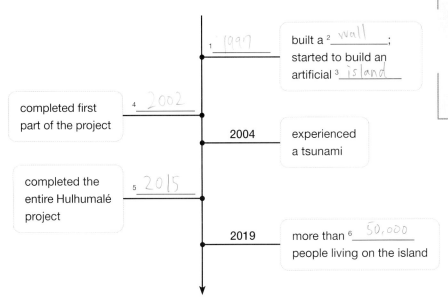

1 _1997_

built a ² _wall_ ; started to build an artificial ³ _island_

⁴ _2002_
completed first part of the project

2004 experienced a tsunami

⁵ _2015_
completed the entire Hulhumalé project

2019 more than ⁶ _50,000_ people living on the island

E ▶ **LISTEN FOR DETAILS** Watch Segment 2 of the presentation. Circle the correct answers.

1. If all of the ice in the world melted, sea levels would rise by **66 / 106** meters.

2. According to the World Bank, at least **35 / 55** countries have lost land area because of rising sea levels.

3. Scientists predict that it might take **3,500 / 5,000** years for all of Earth's ice to melt.

AFTER VIEWING

F **APPLY** Work with a partner. Discuss the questions below.

1. Besides affecting our communities, what other effects do rising sea levels have on the environment? Think of two examples.

2. What is one thing people can do to help slow down global warming?

A model of the Hulhumalé project

Noticing Language

LISTEN FOR LANGUAGE *Express cause and effect*

A Read the sentences below. Underline the words and phrases that signal causes and effects.

> **Communication Skill**
> **Expressing Cause and Effect**
> Describing cause-and-effect relationships helps listeners understand how or why something happened, as well as the results of the event.

1. The increase in rainfall will cause floods.

2. How will climate change affect your community?

3. A change in our behavior now may help reduce the impact of climate change.

4. Most scientists believe that sea levels will rise as a result of global warming.

5. The effects of higher sea levels will be stronger in some parts of the world.

6. Global warming is a consequence of human behavior.

B 🎧 Listen to the following excerpts from the presentation in Lesson B. Complete the sentences with the words you hear.

1. "Maybe it seems as if most of the _____ of climate change is in the future."

2. "Some places around the world, however, are already in real danger from the _____ of climate change."

3. "Any increase in the sea level could therefore _____ dangerous floods."

4. "Scientists predict that global warming will _____ the sea level to rise by more than a meter by the end of this century."

5. "And how would that _____ our world?"

C Work with a partner. Is the text in **bold** a cause or an effect in each sentence? Check (✓).

	Cause	Effect
1. The increase in rainfall will cause **floods**.	✓	
2. **Global warming** is a consequence of human behavior.		✓
3. **A change in the temperature of the ocean water** can affect the plants and animals living it.		✓
4. Most scientists predict **a rise in sea levels** as a result of global warming.	✓	
5. **Natural disasters such as volcanic eruptions** can lead to changes in the average global temperature.	✓	

Doha, Qatar, at night. With more of the world's population living in cities, our night sky is becoming brighter.

D 🎧 Listen to a short talk about the impact of human activities on the environment. Complete the cause-and-effect chains with the correct answers. Then use cause-and-effect words and phrases to describe these events to your partner.

1.

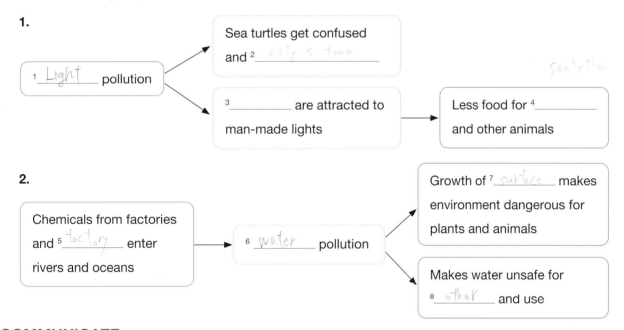

¹ _Light_ pollution

Sea turtles get confused and ² _city is town_

³ _____ are attracted to man-made lights

Less food for ⁴ _____ and other animals

seatrtle

2.

Chemicals from factories and ⁵ _factory_ enter rivers and oceans

⁶ _water_ pollution

Growth of ⁷ _surface_ makes environment dangerous for plants and animals

Makes water unsafe for ⁸ _other_ and use

COMMUNICATE

E Choose one of the topics below and make notes about the possible effects of the trend.

An increase in ...
- international travel
- the use of plastic
- the use of wind and solar energy
- the number of university graduates

F Work with a partner. Take turns explaining some of the possible effects of the trend.

> An increase in international travel will lead to an increase in jobs.
> But it will also cause many tourist destinations to be overcrowded.

Communicating Ideas

LEARNING OBJECTIVES

- Use appropriate language for expressing cause and effect
- Collaborate to raise awareness about an environmental problem

ASSIGNMENT

Task: You are going to collaborate in a group to design a campaign to raise awareness about an environmental problem.

LISTEN FOR INFORMATION

A 🎧 **LISTEN FOR MAIN IDEAS** Listen to a discussion by members of the Environmental Club. Check (✓) the kinds of issues that the students are facing at their college.

1. ☐ energy waste

2. ☐ single-use plastics

3. ☐ difficulty in recycling

4. ☐ food waste

B 🎧 **LISTEN FOR DETAILS** Listen again. Take notes on the causes of the issues the students discussed.

Issues	Cause(s)

C Think of some possible ways to address the issues. Note your ideas below.

_____

_____

_____

_____

_____

_____

COLLABORATE

D Work in a group. Imagine you are part of the Environmental Club. Design a campaign focusing on one of the issues in Exercise A. Come up with a few actions that your campaign will urge students or the college to take. Use the chart to help you.

Campaign focus	
Campaign slogan	
Actions needed	
How the actions will help	

E Share your campaign idea with another group. Explain how your campaign is going to raise awareness of the issue and help improve the school environment.

> The aim of our campaign is to reduce the amount of food waste in our school.

> There are a few actions we can all take. First, we would like to urge the cafeteria management team to consider making the serving sizes of the food smaller.

Checkpoint

Reflect on what you have learned. Check your progress.

I can ...   understand and use words related to climate change.

current	effect	flood	melt	ordinary
predict	protect	require	rise	suffer

use noun and verb word forms.

watch and understand a presentation about the impact of climate change.

use a timeline to take notes.

listen for time signals.

notice language for describing cause and effect.

use language to express cause and effect.

collaborate and communicate effectively to raise awareness about an environmental issue.

Part of a rainforest being cleared in Iguaçu National Park, Brazil

UNIT
5
E F
G H

Building Vocabulary

LEARN KEY WORDS

A 🎧 Listen to and read the passage below. What is one impact of deforestation? Discuss with a partner.

> **Protecting the Lungs of the Earth**
>
> Today we are **witnessing** a **global** crisis—deforestation. South America and Africa, in particular, have experienced **massive** deforestation in just a few decades. The **loss** of these forests is caused mainly by natural disasters—like forest fires and storms—and by human activities like mining and the **development** of **land** for farming and houses. One of the most **extreme** examples of deforestation is in the Amazon, where some of the largest and most important forests are located. If you compare photos from just 20 years ago and today, it is easy to see the **absence** of green spaces. We have already lost about one-third of the Earth's forests, and this has had a serious impact on climate change. When forests are cut down, the **carbon** that is stored in the trees is released into the air as carbon dioxide. As of 2019, carbon dioxide from deforestation made up 11% of global greenhouse gas emissions. Saving existing forests is one effective way to **reduce** the amount of carbon dioxide we put into the air.

B Work with a partner. Discuss the questions below.

1. Look at the photo on the previous page. Why do you think the rainforest is being cleared?

2. The negative consequences of deforestation are well-known. But why do you think it still happens?

C Match the correct form of each word in **bold** from Exercise A with its meaning.

1. _____ to see something happen

2. _____ an area of ground

3. _____ very large

4. _____ to make smaller

5. _____ a chemical element

6. _____ involving the entire world

7. _____ the fact that something is not there

8. _____ the state of no longer having something

9. _____ greater than usual or expected

10. _____ the building of new homes, roads, bridges, etc.

D Complete the chart below with the correct words.

Verb	Noun
	development
	loss
reduce	
witness	

E Complete the sentences with the correct form of the words in Exercise D.

1. There were several _____ to last night's accident.

2. The community has opposed plans to _____ the area. The residents do not want shops and hotels there.

3. A _____ in the use of fossil fuels is an important step to protect the environment.

4. If we don't fight for this land, we will _____ it forever.

COMMUNICATE

F Write an example for each prompt below.

1. one way to reduce your carbon footprint (your impact on the environment)

   _____

2. a global issue that you are concerned about

   _____

3. something important you lost

   _____

4. the most extreme weather you've experienced

   _____

G Work with a partner. Take turns sharing your examples in Exercise F. Respond to your partner's ideas or ask follow-up questions.

> I think one way of reducing my carbon footprint is by saving energy, such as turning off the lights when they're not in use.

> I agree. I enjoy nice long baths, but I think I should try to take short showers instead!

> Well, that would certainly save water!

Viewing and Note-taking

LEARNING OBJECTIVES

- Watch and understand a talk about a response to an environmental problem
- Notice intonation for finished and unfinished thoughts

TEDTALKS

Yvonne Aki-Sawyerr is from Freetown, the capital city of Sierra Leone. She has been active in promoting development in her city that will not harm the environment. In her TED Talk, *The City Planting a Million Trees in Two Years*, Aki-Sawyerr discusses her plans to improve the quality of life in her city.

BEFORE VIEWING

A Read a description of Aki-Sawyerr's experience before she began her project. Why do you think she was shocked? Discuss your ideas with a partner.

> In December 2015, Yvonne Aki-Sawyerr was driving on the outskirts of the capital city in Sierra Leone. She hadn't really paid attention to her surroundings whenever she drove by. But one day, she was shocked when she realized that something was very different from 18 months ago.

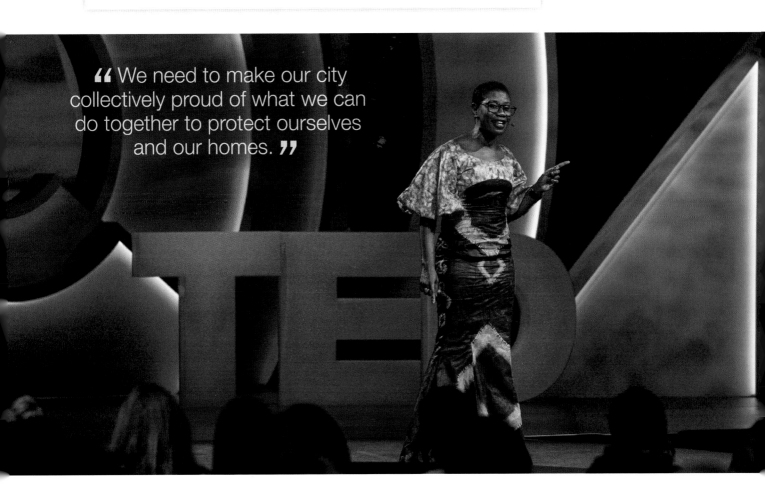

" We need to make our city collectively proud of what we can do together to protect ourselves and our homes. **"**

WHILE VIEWING

B ▶ **LISTEN FOR MAIN IDEAS** Watch Yvonne Aki-Sawyerr's TED Talk. For each statement, write **T** for true or **F** for false.

1. _____ Aki-Sawyerr was shocked that the forests in her city had disappeared.

2. _____ In the last 20 years, fewer and fewer people in Freetown live in informal housing.

3. _____ Aki-Sawyerr's goal is to increase the amount of greenery in her city by 70%.

4. _____ Aki-Sawyerr's plan has started to show some positive results.

C ▶ **LISTEN FOR DETAILS** Watch Aki-Sawyerr's TED Talk again. Complete the notes in the timeline.

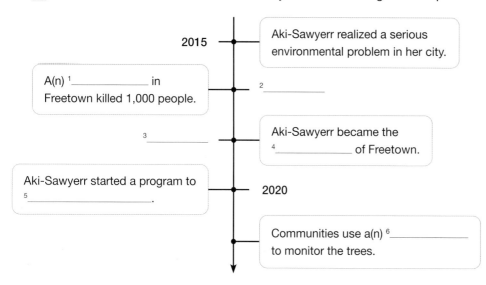

2015 — Aki-Sawyerr realized a serious environmental problem in her city.

A(n) ^{1}_____ in Freetown killed 1,000 people. — ^{2}_____

^{3}_____ — Aki-Sawyerr became the ^{4}_____ of Freetown.

Aki-Sawyerr started a program to ^{5}_____. — 2020

Communities use a(n) ^{6}_____ to monitor the trees.

D **IDENTIFY CAUSE AND EFFECT** Work with a partner. Complete the cause-and-effect chain by putting the events in the correct order. Then take turns using signal phrases for cause-and-effect to describe these events to your partner.

1. a. crop failure
   b. bad weather
   c. people move from farms to cities

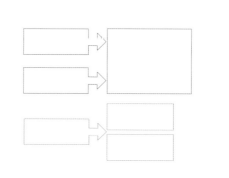

2. a. deforestation
   b. pressure to build houses
   c. lack of development control

3. a. protection against landslides
   b. increase in biodiversity
   c. plant trees

WORDS IN THE TALK
biodiversity (n) the number and types of plants and animals in an environment
carbon sink (n) anything that absorbs more carbon from the atmosphere than it releases
landslide (n) a huge amount of earth falling down the side of a mountain
mourn (v) to feel or express great sadness
surroundings (n) the area around a person
water catchment (n) an area where water is collected by the natural landscape

AFTER VIEWING

E SUMMARIZE Complete the summary using the words in the box.

forests	buildings	climate change	landslide	program

One day in 2015, when Yvonne Aki-Sawyerr looked around her city, she realized she was witnessing the effects of [1] _____. The green spaces were all gone. The hills had no more [2] _____. Instead, they were covered with [3] _____. Without the trees to hold the earth in place, there was a terrible [4] _____. Aki-Sawyerr wanted to do something, so she decided to run for mayor of the city. As mayor, she began a [5] _____ to plant one million trees in two years. Many people in Freetown took part in the program. Aki-Sawyerr hopes it will prevent landslides and make Freetown green and beautiful again.

PRONUNCIATION *Finished and unfinished thoughts*

F 🎧 Listen to the excerpt from the TED Talk. Notice how the speaker's voice pitch goes up or down to show whether her thoughts are finished.

It was December 2015, a month since the end of the Ebola outbreak in Sierra Leone, and I was driving along the Grafton Road on the outskirts of our capital city, Freetown. I'd driven along that road so many times over the past 18 months, but honestly, I'd been so preoccupied, I didn't notice my surroundings.

> **Pronunciation Skill**
> **Finished and Unfinished Thoughts**
>
> Speakers use a falling intonation (usually at the end of sentences) to show that a thought is finished. To indicate an unfinished thought, speakers often pause briefly and use a slightly higher pitch at the end of a phrase. Doing this gives listeners time to process the information, and shows more ideas are to come.

G 🎧 Mark where you expect the voice pitch to go up or down in the sentences below. Then listen and check your answers.

1. If we all work together and make changes in our habits, we can slow the effects of climate change.

2. It is difficult to say which is worse—too much rain or too little.

3. When farmers lose their crops, they also often lose their farms and end up moving to the city.

H Mark where the voice pitch should go up or down in the sentences. Then take turns reading the sentences aloud to a partner.

1. Planting new trees won't stop climate change, but it can help prevent floods.

2. One way to reduce plastic use is to bring your own shopping bag.

3. Using clean and renewable energy like solar, wind, and geothermal energy is the best way to decrease the use of fossil fuels.

Thinking Critically

ANALYZE INFORMATION

A Look at the infographic and answer the questions. Discuss the questions below with a partner.

1. What are some examples of e-waste?

_____

2. Look at the different factors leading to the increase of e-waste. Which of these can people improve through changes in their lifestyle?

_____

E-WASTE: A GLOBAL PROBLEM

What happens to the electric and electronic equipment (EEE) that you throw away?
It becomes e-waste. E-waste is a growing problem all over the world.

What's causing the rise in e-waste?

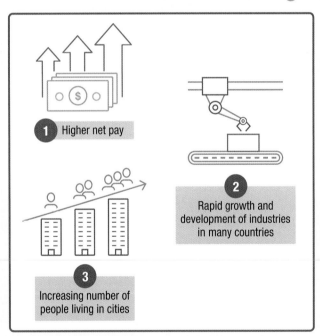

1. Higher net pay

2. Rapid growth and development of industries in many countries

3. Increasing number of people living in cities

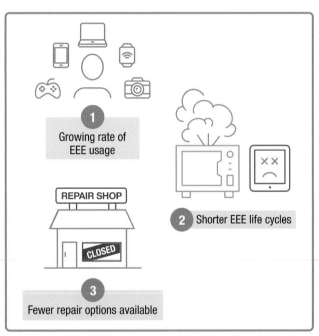

1. Growing rate of EEE usage

REPAIR SHOP
CLOSED

2. Shorter EEE life cycles

3. Fewer repair options available

an increase in the number of EEE bought

a rise in the amount of e-waste

E-WASTE

Source: The International Solid Waste Association (ISWA)

People walk past a wall of mobile phones on the exterior of a mobile phone shop in Japan.

B 🔊 Listen to a podcast about e-waste. For each statement, write **T** (true), **F** (false), or **NG** (not given) if there isn't enough information.

1. _____ The increase in e-waste has started to slow down.

2. _____ E-waste causes pollution in the air, land, and water.

3. _____ The first e-waste recycling system was implemented in Singapore.

4. _____ Different countries are using Switzerland's e-waste recycling system as a model.

5. _____ Singapore has successfully reduced its amount of e-waste.

C Work with a partner. Discuss the questions below.

1. What do you usually do with a cell phone or computer when you no longer need it?

2. Is it easy to recycle electric and electronic equipment in your community?

COMMUNICATE *Synthesize and evaluate ideas*

D How are the ideas in Aki-Sawyerr's TED Talk and the podcast in Exercise B similar? In what ways are they different? Complete the chart below with information from Lesson F and Exercise B.

	Freetown, Sierra Leone	**Singapore**
1. What problem are the people there facing?		
2. What effect(s) does the problem have on the environment?		
3. What action has the government taken?		

E Work with a partner. Discuss the questions below.

1. Which of the approaches above do you think would be useful to your community? Why?

2. What are some other ways we could respond to the environmental issues in Exercise D?

Putting It Together

LEARNING OBJECTIVES

• Research, plan, and present on ways to respond to an environmental problem
• Conclude a presentation with a strong ending

ASSIGNMENT

Group presentation: Your group is going to give a presentation on ways to address an environmental problem in your community.

PREPARE

A Review the unit. Compare the three environmental problems that were presented. What are some of the causes and impacts of these problems?

| Sea level rise (Lesson B) | Deforestation (Lesson F) | E-waste (Lesson G) |

B Work with your group. Choose one of the environmental issues above or your own idea. Do some research about how your community is responding to this issue. Make some notes below.

_____

_____

_____

_____

C Plan your presentation. Use the chart below to help you.

Environmental issue	
Cause of issue	
Measure(s) taken to address the problem	
Idea for improving the measure(s)	

D Look back at the vocabulary, pronunciation, and communication skills you've learned in this unit. What can you use in your presentation? Note any useful language below.

_____

_____

_____

_____

E Below are some ways to end a presentation. Think about how you can include a strong ending in your presentation and add that to your plan.

- Give a summary of your ideas
- Connect your ideas to listeners' lives
- Make a prediction
- Ask a question
- Make a suggestion

> **Presentation Skill**
> **End Strong**
>
> Having a strong ending to your presentation will make listeners more likely to remember your ideas. In Yvonne Aki-Sawyerr's TED Talk, she describes the benefits of her plan and ends by asking the audience to consider taking action.

F Practice your presentation. Make use of the presentation skill that you've learned.

PRESENT

G Give your presentation to another group. Watch their presentation and evaluate them using the Presentation Scoring Rubrics at the back of the book.

H Discuss your evaluation with the other group. Give feedback on two things they did well and two areas for improvement.

Checkpoint

Reflect on what you have learned. Check your progress.

I can ... understand and use words to talk about environmental change.

absence	**carbon**	**development**	**extreme**	**global**
land	**loss**	**massive**	**reduce**	**witness**

use noun and verb word forms.

watch and understand a talk about a response to an environmental problem.

notice intonation for finished and unfinished thoughts.

interpret an infographic about e-waste.

synthesize and evaluate different solutions to environmental problems.

conclude a presentation with a strong ending.

give a presentation about ways to address an environmental problem.

"Hello World!," an audiovisual
exhibit that features thousands of
video diaries posted online

6

Our Digital Life

Q **How can we protect ourselves online?**

The artwork in the photo is titled "Hello World!". Created by artist Christopher Baker, it features 5,000 video diaries posted online, and shows people's desire to share their stories with the world. It represents what people are increasingly doing today. As we shop, play games, or chat online, we share information about ourselves. This, however, increases our risk of encountering crime online. In this unit, we'll look at ways to keep our personal information safe.

THINK and DISCUSS

1 Look at the photo and read the caption. What activities do you do online? Which of these involve sharing information about yourself?

2 Look at the essential question and the unit introduction. Do you worry about the safety of your information online? Why, or why not?

Building Vocabulary

LEARN KEY WORDS

A 🎧 Listen to and read the information below. Is the information surprising to you? Why, or why not? Discuss with a partner.

The Rise in Cybercrime

A cybercrime is a **crime** carried out using computers or the internet. In 2021, cybercrime cost the global economy about six trillion USD, and the number is expected to **increase** in the future. What's causing this? First, the number of internet **users** is growing, which means there are more opportunities for **criminals**. Second, technology is evolving—and so are criminals. They use software programs to send email **attachments** containing computer viruses, or spread harmful **links** through social media. They also target social media **accounts** to steal users' **personal** information and **identities**. So it's important to be alert when doing anything online—one **careless** move could lead to a cyberattack!

THE COST OF CYBERCRIMES

71.1 million
Number of people who fall victim to cybercrimes yearly

$13 million
Global cybercrime damages per second

$4.2 billion
Internet crime victim losses in 2020

$1.85 million
Average cost of a ransomware attack

$190,000
Average cost of cybercrime for organizations

Sources: FBI; Sophos; Cybersecurity Ventures; Accenture Finances Online Review For Business

B Match the correct form of each word in **bold** in Exercise A with its meaning.

1. _____ an illegal activity
2. _____ to become greater in number
3. _____ related to a specific individual
4. _____ a person who does things that are against the law
5. _____ someone who uses a product, machine, or service
6. _____ facts or information about a person that defines who they are
7. _____ not paying enough attention to something, causing mistakes
8. _____ a record of your information kept by an organization or a company
9. _____ a separate file that is included and sent with an electronic message
10. _____ a connection that leads you to something else online

C Words with suffixes *-ful* and *-less* sometimes have opposite meanings. Complete the chart with the correct form of the words. Then complete the sentences using the most suitable words.

Word	*-ful*	*-less*
care		careless
color	colorful	
hope	hopeful	
thought		thoughtless
use	useful	

1. All the children wore _____ costumes for the performance.
2. The house was filled with broken, _____ old junk.
3. The tea is still hot, so be _____ when you drink.
4. Without a solution, the situation felt _____.
5. Thank you so much for the personalized gift. It was very _____ of you.

D Complete the passage using the correct form of the words in **bold** from Exercise A.

In 2021, LinkedIn—a business networking site—experienced a cyberattack that affected about 700 million of its [1]_____. The [2]_____, known as "God User," hacked into customers' [3]_____ and posted the stolen information on a forum. The hacker revealed that they had access to [4]_____ information like email addresses, phone numbers, and other social media details. This information would allow other hackers to create convincing fake [5]_____. LinkedIn has warned users to be wary of suspicious messages or phone calls.

COMMUNICATE

E Work with a partner. Discuss the questions below.

1. Where do you store your personal information like account numbers and passwords?
2. What do you do when you receive messages that contain links? Do you usually click on them?

Viewing and Note-taking

LEARNING OBJECTIVES

• Watch a video podcast about online fraud
• Take notes using key terms
• Listen for rhetorical questions

BEFORE VIEWING

A 🎧 Listen to an excerpt from a talk about fraud. Write the key term and then add details in the chart below.

Key Term	Details/Examples

> **Note-taking Skill**
> **Taking Notes Using Key Terms**
>
> When you listen to a lecture, talk, or podcast, you can organize your notes around key terms. Speakers usually repeat key terms and define or explain them with examples or more details. Noting the key terms can help you review new concepts and ideas more easily.

B You are going to watch a video podcast about one type of cybercrime. Have you experienced a cybercrime or heard about someone's experience of it? What was it? Discuss with a partner and note your ideas.

_____

_____

_____

WHILE VIEWING

C ▶ **LISTEN FOR RHETORICAL QUESTIONS** Watch the video podcast about online fraud. Note the rhetorical questions the speaker used.

1. _____ ?

2. _____ ?

3. _____ ?

4. _____ ?

> **Listening Skill**
> **Listening for Rhetorical Questions**
>
> Sometimes speakers ask questions, but they don't expect an answer. Instead, they often answer the question themselves. These are called rhetorical questions. Speakers use rhetorical questions to get listeners' attention and to signal an important idea.

D **LISTEN FOR MAIN IDEAS** Look at the rhetorical questions you noted in Exercise C. Check (✓) the two statements that best describe the speaker's main ideas.

a. ☐ Cybercriminals often target people who share a lot of content online.

b. ☐ Cybercriminals have many ways to trick people into giving away their personal information.

c. ☐ Being more careful with the links and attachments you click on is one way to prevent pharming.

d. ☐ We can protect ourselves from internet fraud by being more careful with our personal information.

E ▶ **LISTEN FOR KEY TERMS** Watch Segment 1 of the video podcast. Complete the notes with explanations of the key terms. Write no more than three words for each answer.

Key Terms	Explanation
Online fraud	when criminals make use of your [1]_____ to steal your money
Phishing	when you [2]_____ that asks for your personal information
Pharming	when criminals direct you to [3]_____ where they can access your personal information

F ▶ **LISTEN FOR DETAILS** Watch Segment 2 of the video podcast. Check (✓) the advice the speaker gives for preventing online fraud.

a. ☐ Make sure your password is not obvious.

b. ☐ Keep your account secure by using a two-step login process.

c. ☐ Delete emails that have links in them.

d. ☐ Check URLs to confirm that they are correctly spelled.

e. ☐ Avoid accessing your personal accounts when connected to a public Wi-Fi network.

AFTER VIEWING

G **REFLECT** Work with a partner. Discuss the questions below.

1. Have you received phishing emails or suspicious links? How did you know they weren't real?

2. When asked to provide your personal information online, what do you usually do?

3. Why do you think people use weak passwords or take other risks with their personal information?

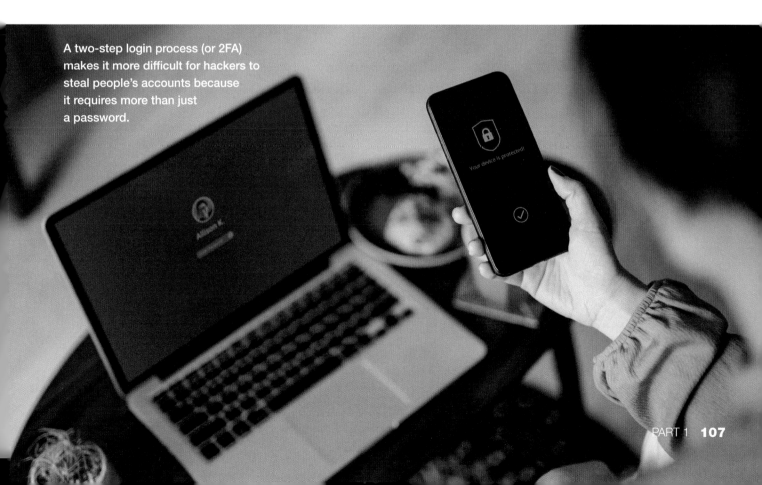

A two-step login process (or 2FA) makes it more difficult for hackers to steal people's accounts because it requires more than just a password.

Noticing Language

LISTEN FOR LANGUAGE *Use examples to support ideas*

A Below are some ways to give examples when explaining ideas. Where do these phrases usually appear in a sentence—at the beginning, in the middle, or both are possible? Discuss with a partner.

1. for example

2. such as

3. to give an example

4. like

5. say

6. for instance

7. an example of this is

8. an example that you may know is

> ### Communication Skill
> **Using Examples to Support Ideas**
>
> Examples are an effective way to explain and support ideas. Speakers often introduce their examples using certain words and phrases. They may use general expressions like "for example," or they may use adjectives to give more information about the example and show how it's linked to their idea.

B The expression "a(n) _____ example is …" can be used with different adjectives to give more information about the example. Check (✓) the adjectives that are suitable.

a. ☐ great   **b.** ☐ fast   **c.** ☐ common

d. ☐ recent   **e.** ☐ famous   **f.** ☐ big

C 🎧 Listen to the following excerpts from the video podcast in Lesson B. Complete the sentences with the expressions the speaker used to give examples.

1. "Or, _____, they get your birthday, national identity number, and driver's license number."

2. "_____ forms of online fraud are phishing and pharming."

3. "Here, criminals create a website that looks almost exactly like a real one— _____, an online store, your bank, or a government office."

4. "They use Wi-Fi that is not secure, in places _____ coffee shops and airports."

5. "If you need to share personal information _____ a credit card number, make sure you are on a secure website."

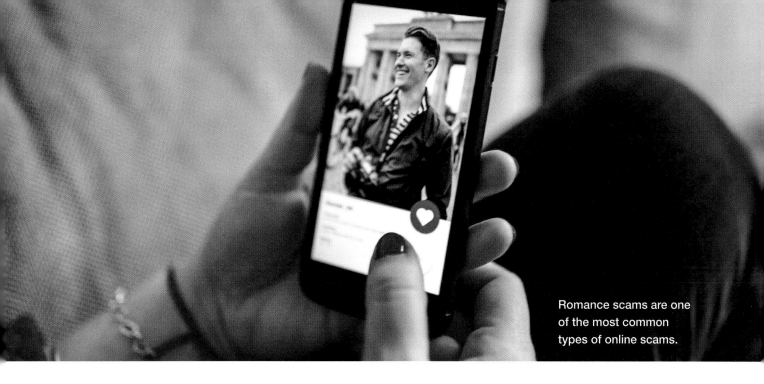

Romance scams are one of the most common types of online scams.

D 🎧 Listen to a talk about cybercrime and circle **T** for true or **F** for false.

1. In 2021, most of the victims were a result of social engineering scams.   **T**   **F**

2. Scammers in social engineering scams get people to commit crimes for them.   **T**   **F**

3. Scammers steal personal information by pretending to be people or companies the victims are familiar with, or by creating false emergencies.   **T**   **F**

E 🎧 Listen again. Write the examples that the speaker gave to support the ideas below.

Idea	Examples
People scammers may pretend to be	
Brands scammers pose as	
Types of social engineering scams	

COMMUNICATE

F Work with a partner. Choose a term or topic each from the box below to explain. Think of at least one example to support your explanation.

personal information	identity theft	social engineering scam

G Take turns explaining the term or topic you chose. Include example(s) in your explanation.

Communicating Ideas

LEARNING OBJECTIVES

- Use appropriate language for giving examples
- Collaborate to discuss ways to stay safe online

ASSIGNMENT

Task: You are going to collaborate in a group to promote online safety by giving tips on how to stay safe.

LISTEN FOR INFORMATION

A 🎧 Take a quiz on online safety below. For each scenario, decide whether the action is Safe or Risky. Then listen and check your answers.

1. Melvin gets an email saying that he has won a prize from a lucky draw. He clicks on the link that takes him to a bank's website.	**Safe**	**Risky**
2. Cheryl uses her friend's computer to check her bank account.	**Safe**	**Risky**
3. Lee is at a café and uses the free Wi-Fi to pay his electricity bill.	**Safe**	**Risky**
4. Helen receives an urgent email from her boss asking her to send him a list of customers' contact information. She calls him to ask about his request.	**Safe**	**Risky**
5. Mrs. Cho receives a message from someone who says he's a family member. He asks for money because he has lost his phone. She sends the person some money.	**Safe**	**Risky**
6. Rina receives a text from the post office saying that her package can't be delivered until she pays a fee. She doesn't respond because she didn't buy anything.	**Safe**	**Risky**
7. Bryan receives an email from his cell phone company saying there's a problem with his account statement. He downloads the attachment to see what the issue is.	**Safe**	**Risky**
8. Simon gets a text message from the national department of health. It states that more information (full name, address, etc.) is needed to keep his identification number active. He deletes the text.	**Safe**	**Risky**

B Work with a partner. For the scenarios that are risky, discuss what the person should do instead and the reasons for it. Make notes.

_____

_____

_____

_____

COLLABORATE

C Work in a group. Brainstorm some ways people can protect themselves online. Make notes in the left column of the chart below.

Tips to stay safe	Scenario
Check the identity of anyone who asks for your personal information.	You receive a call from someone who says he's a police officer. The officer says he needs your passport number to investigate a crime.

D Think of an example scenario to explain each tip. You can use the ideas in Exercises A and B, or your own ideas. Complete the right column of the chart.

E Share your tips for staying safe online with another group. Explain and support your ideas using the example scenarios.

> It's important to check someone's identity before giving any personal information. For example, if you receive a call …

> You should also take note of …

Checkpoint

Reflect on what you have learned. Check your progress.

I can …   understand and use words related to cybercrime.

| account | attachment | careless | crime | criminal |
| identity | increase | link | personal | user |

use suffixes -ful and -less.

watch and understand a video podcast about online fraud.

take notes on key terms.

listen for rhetorical questions.

notice language for giving examples.

explain and support ideas using examples.

collaborate and communicate effectively to raise awareness about online safety.

Visitors take a selfie in a
ball pit at the Supercandy
Pop-Up Museum.

Building Vocabulary

LEARN KEY WORDS

A 🎧 Listen to and read the passage below. Why is it important we pay attention to our digital footprint? Discuss with a partner.

> **Our Digital Footprint**
>
> When you meet people for the first time, you can control the way you look and what you say. But what about something you have said or done online? Do you know that many **employers** review job applicants' social media posts in their hiring process? The **trail** of **data** you leave when using the internet—for example, the websites you visit and the emails you send—is your **digital** footprint. You might not be aware of how your digital footprint affects real life, but in fact, it can really matter. James Gunn, an American filmmaker and actor, was fired from his project because people found some of his old social media **posts** offensive. Similarly, Yoshiro Mori, president of the Tokyo Olympic organizing committee, had to leave his position after some **comments** he had made during an online meeting were thought to be sexist. While it's clear that famous people have to be careful with what they say or do online, it's also important for every internet user to pay attention to their digital footprint.

B Work with a partner. Discuss the questions below.

1. The photo on the previous page shows the Supercandy Pop-Up Museum in Germany. The museum has many different colorful sets for visitors to take interesting selfies and videos for posting on social media. Do you often take selfies and videos and share them online?

2. How often do you update your social media status or comment on your friends' posts online?

3. Do you ever delete old posts? Why, or why not?

C Match the correct form of each word in **bold** from Exercise A with its meaning.

1. _____ a note expressing an opinion

2. _____ relating to computers or the internet

3. _____ a mark left behind

4. _____ a piece of writing or pictures you share online

5. _____ information

6. _____ someone that people work for

D Read the sentences below. Choose the options that are closest to the meaning of the words in **bold**.

1. If you close the curtains, you will have more **privacy.**
   a. personal space without attention from other people
   b. room to move around

2. When the weather is good, the mountains are **visible** from the city.
   a. hidden from view
   b. able to be seen

3. He is a **professional** actor and has starred in many movies.
   a. full-time
   b. very popular

4. The second book offers an **extension** of the ideas in the first book.
   a. application
   b. expansion or continuation

E Complete the chart with the correct words.

Noun	Verb	Adjective
extension		
privacy	–	
	–	professional
	–	visible

F Complete the sentences using the correct form of the words from Exercise E.

1. Her employer is going to _____ her contract for one more year.

2. Pop stars and movie stars are often followed by the media and have little _____ in their lives.

3. I need glasses because my _____ is poor.

4. It is important to be _____ at a job interview. Make sure you have all the documents you may need.

COMMUNICATE

G Work with a partner. Discuss the questions below.

1. What kind of professional work would you like to do in the future?

2. What do you do to protect your privacy online?

3. When you are online, many companies try to collect data about your behavior. What data do you think they already have about you?

Viewing and Note-taking

LEARNING OBJECTIVES

- Watch and understand a talk about managing one's digital footprint
- Notice contrastive stress

Amber Case is an anthropologist who studies the interaction between human beings and machines, especially computers. She is interested in how the impact of technology on our culture and social lives is increasing. In her talk, *Our Online Selves*, she offers advice on managing our digital footprint.

BEFORE VIEWING

A Read the information below and discuss the questions with a partner.

> Your digital self is the persona you use when you're online. It includes your online behavior, online voice, and online presentation. Posting regularly on social media is an online behavior. What you say and how you say it when you post online is your online voice. And how you would like others to see you is your online presentation. Unlike in real life, you can have more than one online persona.

1. What is your digital self like? Think of some examples of your online behavior and your online voice that contribute to your online persona.

2. Do you act differently online and offline? Why, or why not?

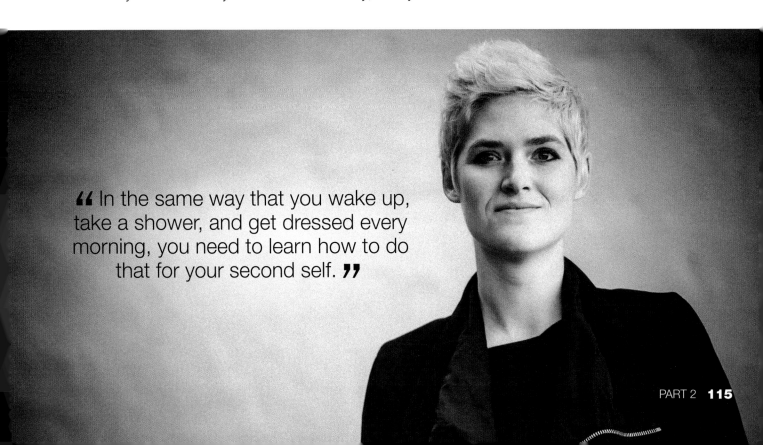

❝ In the same way that you wake up, take a shower, and get dressed every morning, you need to learn how to do that for your second self. ❞

WHILE VIEWING

B ▶ **LISTEN FOR MAIN IDEAS** Watch Amber Case's talk and choose the main idea.

    a. Social media can cause problems for your social life and your career.

    b. Computers and social media are extensions of our lives in the digital world.

    c. Online communication tools are useful, but they must be managed carefully.

    d. Communication has changed dramatically in just one generation.

C ▶ **LISTEN FOR RHETORICAL QUESTIONS** Complete the rhetorical questions Case used. Then match each rhetorical question to its purpose. The first question is done for you.

makes a suggestion	gives a warning
tells you a definition is coming next	

    1. Question: But what is _____ a cyborg _____ ?

      Purpose: It _____ .

    2. Question: What if a status update stops you _____ ?

      Purpose: It _____ .

    3. Question: Are there any photos _____ ?

      Purpose: It _____ .

D ▶ **LISTEN FOR KEY TERMS** Watch Segment 1 of Case's talk. Use the chart below to note important details of the key terms she discusses.

Key Terms	Details / Explanation
Cyborg anthropologist	a person who studies how humans interact with [1]_____ , and how it affects [2]_____
Cyborg	a person who [3]_____ to adapt to a new environment, e.g., [4]_____
Second self	our digital selves with all the information we [5]_____

E ▶ **SUMMARIZE** Watch Segment 2 of Case's talk. Complete the summary of her advice.

    1. Check your _____ , so that your posts cannot be seen by _____ .

    2. Check your _____ , _____ and _____ . Is there anything that you don't want other people to see, now or in the future?

    3. If you want to share all kinds of information freely, you should consider having a(n) _____ that uses _____ .

WORDS IN THE TALK
digital footprint (n) the trail of data you leave when using the internet
hammer (n) a tool used to fasten nails

AFTER VIEWING

F REFLECT Work with a partner. Discuss the questions below.

1. Do you agree that people should have different social media accounts for different purposes?
2. Do you "curate" the content that you share on your social media accounts? Why, or why not?

PRONUNCIATION *Contrastive stress*

G  Listen to the excerpts from the talk. Underline the words that Case stresses for contrast.

1. "Anthropologists study human relationships. Cyborg anthropologists study humans and technology and how technology affects culture."
2. "Just as a hammer is an extension of your fist and a knife is an extension of your teeth, a computer could be considered an extension of your mind."

> ### Pronunciation Skill
> **Contrastive Stress**
>
> In regular sentence stress, speakers usually emphasize the content words in order to draw attention to the main ideas in the sentence. In contrastive stress, speakers place extra stress on certain words to compare or contrast different ideas or information.

H Read the sentences below and underline the words or phrases that receive contrastive stress. Then listen and check your answers.

1. Is this your phone or is it that one?
2. The first item is selling at regular price, but the second one gets 50 percent off.
3. I thought this was my notebook, but later realized it was my classmate's.
4. **A:** Did you see Jenny's post from yesterday?

   B: I saw the one on Friday.
5. **A:** Professor Gomez's lecture is starting at nine.

   B: Actually that's Professor Miller's class.
6. **A:** Online shopping is the best—it's so convenient!

   B: I think it's risky. There are so many online scams these days!

I Work with a partner. Discuss what information is being contrasted in each item in Exercise H.

According to Case, people are cyborgs when they create an extension of themselves through the use of technology.

Thinking Critically

- Interpret an infographic about the impact of our digital footprint
- Synthesize and evaluate advice about managing one's digital footprint

ANALYZE INFORMATION

A Look at the infographic and answer the questions. Discuss your answers with a partner.

1. How many employers use social media to evaluate job seekers? Why do you think they do so?

_____

2. What percentage of the people in the survey experienced negative consequences because of their activities online?

_____

3. How might students be negatively affected by their digital footprint?

_____

Why Should We Care About Our Digital Footprint?

MORE THAN
90% of interviewers are currently using social media as part of their hiring process

21% of interviewers rejected an interviewee after looking them up online

56% of adults surveyed don't actively think about the consequences of their online activities

14% of adults surveyed say they have had negative experiences because of their online activities

Of these:
- 21% were fired from a job
- 16% lost out on a job opportunity
- 16% lost their health insurance
- 15% were turned down for a home loan
- 14% lost out on the college they wanted

Sources: Microsoft, Job Description Library (2022)

B Think about your online activities and behaviors. Check (✓) the statement that best describes you. Then answer the questions below and discuss your ideas with a partner.

☐ **I actively share posts on social media.**

　　1. What do you usually post on social media?

　　2. Do you think about the consequences of your posts? Why, or why not?

☐ **I rarely post on social media. I just read other people's posts.**

　　1. What do your family and friends usually post online?

　　2. Have you heard about someone who had a bad experience because of their online activities? What was it?

C 🎧 Listen to a talk about managing digital footprints. For each statement, choose **T** for true or **F** for false.

1. What we choose to say or do online affects our active digital footprint. **T** **F**

2. Information about when we last visited a website is part of our passive digital footprint. **T** **F**

3. Websites inform users about the kinds of data they collect about them. **T** **F**

4. One way to manage our active digital footprint is to clear cookies often. **T** **F**

COMMUNICATE *Synthesize and evaluate ideas*

D Look at the advice by Amber Case and the speaker in Exercise C on managing your digital footprint. Is each piece of advice useful for managing an active or a passive digital footprint? Check (✓).

	Active	**Passive**
1. Use a nickname online.		
2. Use a VPN when browsing the internet.		
3. Create different work and personal accounts.		
4. Don't share personal information.		
5. Delete cookies from unknown websites.		
6. Update your anti-virus software.		
7. Make sure your posts are visible only to people you know.		

E Look at the advice above. Which of these are you already practicing? Which do you think you will try to do more often? Discuss with a partner.

> I always check the privacy settings of my social media account. I make sure that my posts are only visible to people I already know, and that my account is set to private.

Putting It Together

ASSIGNMENT

Group presentation: Your group is going to do a case study of a type of cybercrime and give a presentation on how people can protect themselves from it.

PREPARE

A Review the unit. Make notes on what the ideas and terms below mean.

Key idea	Notes
Personal information (Lesson B)	
Digital footprint (Lesson E)	
Second self (Lesson F)	

B Work with your group. Choose one of the cybercrimes below or think of your own idea. Search online for information about how the cybercrime works. Note an example of a real incident that happened.

ransomware attacks	hacking	phishing scams	malware

_____

_____

_____

C Plan your presentation. Use the following prompts to help you.

What type of cybercrime is it?	
Who did it happen to?	
What happened as a result?	
What did people do to stop it?	
What lessons can be learned?	

D Look back at the vocabulary, pronunciation, and communication skills you've learned in this unit. What can you use in your presentation? Note any useful language below.

_____

_____

_____

_____

_____

_____

E Below are some ways to introduce and explain concepts. Identify ideas or terms in your presentation that require more explanation. Think about how you can explain them using familiar concepts and add that to your plan.

- Ask a question: *Have you heard of ...?*
- Define it: *Let me explain what I mean by ...*
- Compare it to something familiar: *It's similar to ... / You can think of it in this way ...*

F Practice your presentation. Make use of the presentation skill that you have learned.

> **Presentation Skill**
> **Defining Unfamiliar Concepts**
>
> When speakers talk about ideas that they think are not well-known by their listeners, they can explain them using more familiar concepts. In Amber Case's talk, she explained terms such as "cyborg" by giving a definition and using a recognizable example (an astronaut).

PRESENT

G Give your presentation to another group. Watch their presentation and evaluate them using the Presentation Scoring Rubrics at the back of the book.

H Discuss your evaluation with the other group. Give feedback on two things they did well and two areas for improvement.

Checkpoint

Reflect on what you have learned. Check your progress.

I can ...   understand and use words to talk about digital footprints.

comment	data	digital	employer	extension
post	privacy	professional	trail	visible

☐ use noun, verb, and adjective forms.

☐ watch and understand a talk about managing one's digital footprint.

☐ notice contrastive stress.

☐ interpret an infographic about the impact of our digital footprint.

☐ synthesize and evaluate ideas about managing one's digital footprint.

☐ define and explain unfamiliar terms clearly.

☐ give a presentation on a case study of a cybercrime and how to stay safe.

Tiny houses are usually less than 40 square meters in size and are thought to be eco-friendly.

7

Less Is More

Q **Does having less make us happier?**

Tiny homes like the one in the photo have become popular in recent years. Due to limited space, however, living in a tiny house means living more simply and making changes to one's lifestyle. The idea that having less of something makes us happier may seem strange at first. It's natural to want more of the things we like. But does a bigger house, a second car, or more clothes really bring us more happiness? In this unit, we'll consider whether greater choice leads to greater happiness, and look at advice on how we can live a happier life.

THINK and DISCUSS

1 Look at the photo and read the caption. Would you like to live in a house like this? Why, or why not?

2 Look at the essential question and the unit introduction. Why do you think some people may feel that "less is more"?

Building Vocabulary

LEARN KEY WORDS

A 🎧 Listen to and read the information below. What do you think explains the trend shown in the graph? Discuss with a partner.

Less Choice
Is More

Most people like the idea of **individual** choice. Being able to **choose** gives us a sense of **freedom** and **happiness**: a restaurant that only has one item on the menu is not **likely** to have many customers. But evidence from studies has shown that adding **options** only makes us more **satisfied** to a point. Beyond a certain number of choices, we may no longer experience an increase in happiness. Think, for example, about browsing thousands of movies, TV shows, and songs available online now. With so much choice, making **decisions** has now become a lot harder.

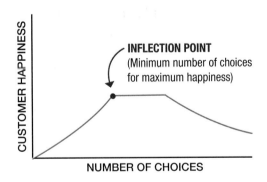

INFLECTION POINT
(Minimum number of choices for maximum happiness)

CUSTOMER HAPPINESS

NUMBER OF CHOICES

Source: Chernev, Böckenholt, and Goodman, "Choice overload: A conceptual review and meta-analysis" (2015)

Many supermarkets have hundreds of **varieties** of items like salad dressing, from **familiar** brands to some we may never have heard of.

B Match the correct form of each word in **bold** in Exercise A with its meaning.

1. _varieties_ different types of something

2. _likely_ expected

3. _familiar_ well-known, common

4. _options_ something that can be chosen

5. _individual_ relating to one person

6. _satisfied_ pleased, content

7. _happiness_ a feeling of joy

8. _freedom_ the ability to do what you want

9. _choose_ to pick something

10. _decisions_ the act or process of deciding something

C Some suffixes can change an adjective to a noun. Use the suffixes below to complete the chart with the correct nouns. Then complete the sentences using the most suitable words.

-ity	-ion	-hood

Adjective	Noun
likely	likelhood
familiar	
satisfied	

1. We were asked to complete a job _____ survey so the company could understand how we felt about our working conditions.

2. Tourists who have visited temples in Japan will be _____ with what Japanese rock gardens look like.

3. Studies show that customers are _____ to make better decisions when fewer options are provided.

D Complete the sentences using the correct form of the words in **bold** from Exercise A.

1. Many people find that they have more _____ when they have a flexible work schedule.

2. Although there aren't many food and drink _____ on the menu, this restaurant does all their dishes really well.

3. Some people believe that to live a happy life, we should learn to be _____ with what we have.

4. My neighborhood library is small but has a good _____ of books.

COMMUNICATE

E Work with a partner. Discuss the questions below.

1. When you go shopping, do you go for brands that you are familiar with or do you try something new?

2. Do you generally prefer to have more or fewer options to choose from? Why?

Viewing and Note-taking

LEARNING OBJECTIVES

• Watch a class discussion about *The Paradox of Choice*
• Record information in a list
• Listen for signal words and phrases

BEFORE VIEWING

A Look at the notes from two students below. Which do you find easier to understand? Why? Discuss with a partner.

Note-taking Skill
Recording Information in a List

When you take notes, it can help to record information using short phrases and lists. Listen for signs that suggest a speaker is going to list information. These can be numbers, words, phrases, or full sentences, for example "first of all" or "I'm going to suggest three ways …" Use a heading and numbers, letters, or bullet points to make clear notes.

Student A

English
• 1.5 billion speakers
• one of the world's most spoken languages

Learning tips
1. Make learning fun → practice with friends
2. Don't be afraid to make mistakes when speaking.
3. Keep a vocabulary notebook.

Student B

There are 1.5 billion speakers of English. It's one of the top languages spoken globally.

Some tips for learning English are practicing with friends to make learning fun, not being afraid of making mistakes when speaking the language, and keeping a vocabulary notebook.

B 🎧 Listen to a short talk. Make notes using lists. Then compare your notes with a partner.

• The KonMar method of Decl
1. be serious about tydying up
2. think about your idea style   kida hase of you living
3. Look thrug all you have and let go of whatever doesn't bring happiness
4. Reflect on what it meant and be gradeful
5. Not room by room but by category (clothe, books, etc)   6. Do easy things first

A variety of yams for sale at a supermarket in Manhattan, New York.

C You are going to watch a class discussion about ideas from a book called *The Paradox of Choice*. A paradox is a statement that seems impossible or untrue because it says two opposite things. An example is the title of this unit, "Less Is More." What ideas do you think you will hear about? Discuss with a partner.

WHILE VIEWING

D ▶ **LISTEN FOR MAIN IDEAS** Watch Segment 1 of the class discussion. What evidence does Schwartz give to support his argument in *The Paradox of Choice*?

   a. The number of options available to consumers today are more than necessary.

   b. People in societies with a lot of wealth and freedom are less happy.

   c. People spend a longer time making decisions because there are too many products with similar features.

> **Listening Skill**
>
> **Listening for Signal Words and Phrases**
>
> Speakers often use words or phrases that signal what they will talk about next. For example, "I'm going to talk about …" introduces a speaker's topic. Words like "first," "second," and "then" help make a speaker's points clearer. Listening for these signals helps you follow and understand what the speaker is talking about.

E ▶ **LISTEN FOR DETAILS** Watch Segment 2 of the class discussion. Complete the notes.

"Maximizers" = want things to be ¹ _absolutely short ____ is best_

"Satisficers" = happy with things that are ² _pretty good_

What to do if you are a maximizer?

1. Be ³ _aware of your personality_

2. Understand that this quality can be ⁴ _____

3. Do something to ⁵ _____

AFTER VIEWING

F **INFER** Are the people in the following scenarios more likely to be a maximizer (M) or a satisficer (S)? Write **M** or **S** for each scenario. Discuss your answers with a partner.

   1. _____ When eating at restaurants, Ari doesn't always look at the entire menu before deciding on what she would like.

   2. _____ Before going on a vacation, Jen always researches the best places to visit and eat for her trip. She often plans in advance and organizes her activities for each day of her trip in a schedule.

   3. _____ When Shen needs help with deciding what to buy, he usually does a quick online search for recommendations. He then chooses something from the list of recommendations.

G **APPLY** Work with a partner. Discuss the questions below.

   1. In what kinds of situations is it better to be a maximizer or a satisficer? Think of one situation for each personality type.

   Maximizer: _____

   Satisficer: _____

   2. Do you think you are more of a maximizer or more of a satisficer? Why?

Noticing Language

LISTEN FOR LANGUAGE *Use signal words to mark transitions*

A Read the signal words and phrases below. When are they used? Match the purposes (a–d) with the signal words (1–4).

> **a.** to introduce a topic
> **b.** to sum up what has been said
> **c.** to organize the ideas
> **d.** to continue or change a topic

> **Communication Skill**
> **Using Signal Words to Mark Transitions**
>
> Some signal words can help you organize your ideas. Others are used to draw listeners' attention to a transition: for example, a new topic, an explanation, or a recap. When you are speaking, include signal words to make it easier for listeners to follow your ideas.

1. __C__ First … / Second … / Then … / Next … / Finally …

2. __a__ To get started … / We're going to … / Let's start with …

3. __b__ Just to recap … / To wrap up … / I think that's all … / I'd like to conclude by …

4. __d__ Now, … / Right, … / So, … / Well, …

B 🎧 Listen to the following excerpts from the class discussion in Lesson B. Complete the sentences with the words you hear. Then discuss with a partner what the speaker did in each excerpt. Use the information in Exercise A to help you.

1. "Today, __We're going to__ discuss the idea that the number of choices people have …"

2. "__So Well__, that is a great example related to the research on how choice impacts individuals."

3. "__Now__ we'll look at two types of personalities that Schwartz talks about in his book—Maximizers and Satisficers."

4. "__Let's start with__ Maximizers."

5. "__First__, just be aware of it. Sometimes, just being aware of your personality type can make life easier."

6. "__Lastly__, do something to reduce your stress level …"

C 🎧 Listen to a talk about FOMO (fear of missing out). Choose the statement that best summarizes the main idea.

a. FOMO marketing is a popular strategy that helps businesses increase their sales.

b. It's important to have a balance of FOMO and JOMO in our lives.

c. Moving from FOMO to JOMO can help people lead happier lives.

Reading is a way to slow down and relax.
This park in Lithuania provides books free
of charge to visitors during the summer.

D 🎧 Listen to the talk again. Complete the notes.

> FOMO = fear of missing out
> • part of many marketing strategies
> • people worry about [1]_____
>   → end up [2]_____
>
> JOMO = [3]_____
> Ways to practice it:
>
> 1. [4]_____.
>
> 2. Reflect on [5]_____.
>
> 3. Practice [6]_____.

COMMUNICATE

E Choose a topic from the box below or think of one of your own. Think of three tips
for your topic and make notes.

How to increase happiness	How to tidy up your house
How to make better decisions	How to learn a foreign language

_____

_____

_____

_____

F Use the words and phrases in Exercise A to organize your ideas. Include an
introduction to your topic.

G Work in a group. Take turns speaking for one minute about your topic.

Communicating Ideas

ASSIGNMENT

Task: You are going to collaborate in a group to examine the advantages and disadvantages of different kinds of personalities.

LISTEN FOR INFORMATION

A 🎧 Are you a maximizer or a satisficer? Listen to a quiz with ten statements. For each statement, score yourself on a scale of 1 (disagree) to 3 (agree).

Personality Quiz

	Disagree	Neutral	Agree
1.	1	(2)	3
2.	1	2	(3)
3.	1	(2)	3
4.	(1)	2	3
5.	1	(2)	3
6.	(1)	2	3
7.	(1)	2	3
8.	1	(2)	3
9.	1	(2)	3
10.	1	2	(3)
		Total score	19

Source: Barry Schwartz et al., "Maximizing Versus Satisficing: Happiness Is a Matter of Choice.," Journal of Personality and Social Psychology 83, no. 5 (2002). Questions are adapted.

B Calculate the total number of points to determine your personality type.

10	11–16	17–23	24–29	30
Extreme satisficer	Satisficer	A little of both	Maximizer	Extreme maximizer

Our personality types can affect the way we make big and small decisions, from choosing a job to shopping for gifts.

COLLABORATE

C Take a class poll. How many students are satisficers, maximizers, or a little of both?

D Work in small groups of people with similar personality types: satisficers, maximizers, and a little of both. Think of and note three advantages or disadvantages of your personality type.

_____

_____

_____

E Choose one or two people from your group to share your ideas with the class.

> The people in my group are satisficers. We'd like to start by sharing the advantages of being a satisficer.

> The first advantage of being a satisficer is being able to make decisions quickly.

Checkpoint

Reflect on what you have learned. Check your progress.

I can ... understand and use words related to making choices.

choose	**decision**	**familiar**	**freedom**	**happiness**
individual	**likely**	**option**	**satisfied**	**variety**

use suffixes to change adjectives to nouns.

watch and understand a class discussion about _The Paradox of Choice_.

record information in a list.

listen for signal words and phrases.

notice signal words that mark transitions.

explain a topic using signal words to organize my ideas.

collaborate and communicate effectively to analyze different personality types.

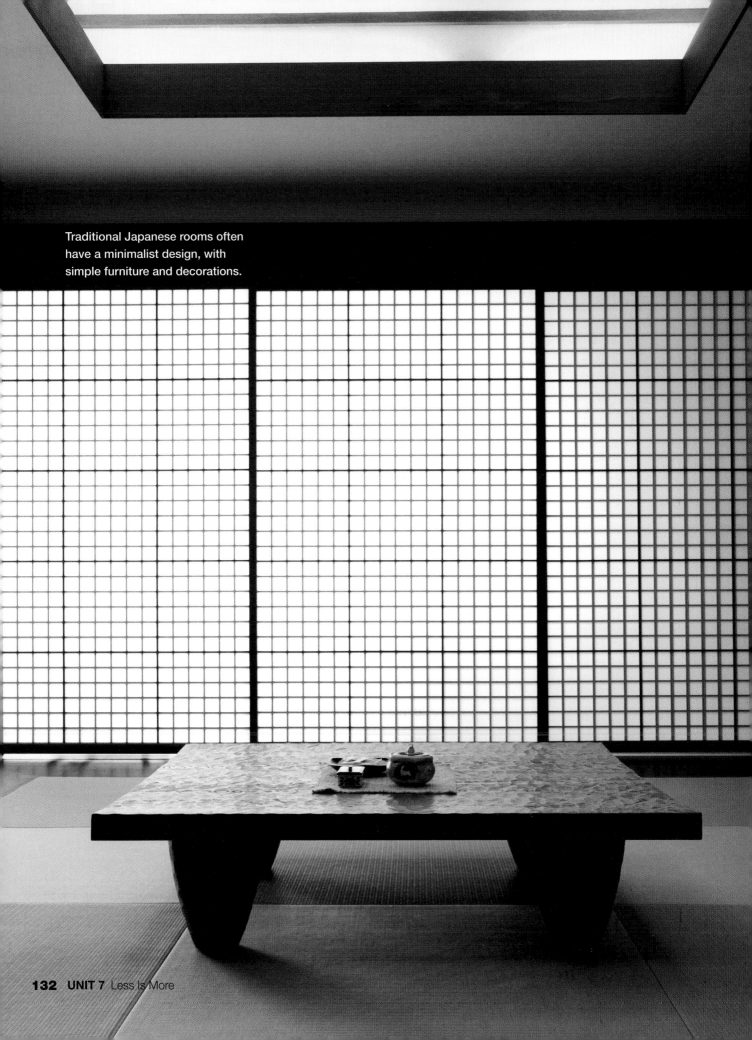

Traditional Japanese rooms often have a minimalist design, with simple furniture and decorations.

Building Vocabulary

LEARNING OBJECTIVES

- Use ten words to talk about the ide
  of minimalism
- Use collocations with *amount*

LEARN KEY WORDS

A 🎧 Listen to and read the passage below. What are some ways people practice the concept of "less is more" in their lives? Discuss with a partner.

> **Downsizing Our Lives**
>
> The phrase "less is more" first appeared in a poem written by Robert Browning in 1855 and was made famous by the 20th-century architect Ludwig Mies van der Rohe. Mies's approach focused on the concept of simplicity. The **majority** of his buildings feature simple lines and a large **amount** of glass; his idea was to make the line between the inside and outside of the building **disappear**.
>
> The idea of "less is more" now influences many people's lifestyles. They realize that living a simpler life brings them more **ease**. Instead of having so many things, more and more people are deciding to get rid of **stuff** they **rarely** use, either by throwing it away or by **digitizing** it. People who do this often say they feel less stressed as a result. The 2020 global pandemic also caused people to change their lifestyles. Many people spent less time shopping and spending and began to rethink what they really needed.

more than half

B Discuss the questions below with a partner.

1. The photo on the previous page is an example of a traditional Japanese room. What does your house or room look like—are there many or few things? How do you feel about your house or room?

2. Have you ever gotten rid of a lot of your stuff? If so, how did you feel afterward? If not, is there anything you could get rid of that might have a positive impact?

C Match the correct form of each word in **bold** from Exercise A with its meaning.

1. _rarely_ not often

2. _ease_ peace and comfort

3. _disapper_ to go away or become impossible to see

4. _digitizing_ to put into a form for use on a computer

5. _stuff_ things, possessions

6. _majority_ more than 50 percent of something

7. _amount_ the quantity of something

D Choose the options that are closest to the meaning of the words in **bold**.

1. In weight measurement, ten kilograms **equals** about 22 pounds.

   a. is the same as   **b.** is greater than

2. Some people have so much stuff it won't even fit in their homes, so they put it into **storage**.

   a. a place for hiding things   **b.** a place for keeping things

3. There's a growing **bunch** of people who value living a simpler and more peaceful life.

   a. team   **b.** group

E The words in the box collocate with the noun **amount**. Complete the sentences using the correct words.

large	small	same
increase	reduce	limited

1. I don't want a(n) _____large_____ amount of money—I'm happy with a simple life.

2. It's worthwhile spending even a(n) _____small_____ amount of time reflecting on what really makes you happy.

3. People can reduce their stress levels if they _____increase_____ the amount of time spent in nature.

4. I think people should spend the _____limited_____ amount of time working and playing.

5. Bringing your own bag when going to the supermarket can help _____same_____ the amount of waste we produce.

6. The team managed to create a stylish dress even though they had a(n) _____reduce_____ amount of materials to work with.

COMMUNICATE

F Write an example next to each prompt below

1. Something you rarely do but your friends often do _____

2. An idea or belief that the majority of your friends share _____

3. Happiness equals … _____

4. The least useful stuff in your room _____

5. Something you can digitize _____

G Work with a partner. Take turns sharing your examples in Exercise F. Explain your choices and discuss any difference or similarities.

Viewing and Note-taking

LEARNING OBJECTIVES

- Watch and understand a talk about the idea of "less is more"
- Notice intonation in yes/no and choice questions

TEDTALKS

Graham Hill is an entrepreneur who studied architecture and design. He is the founder of LifeEdited, a project that helps people design their lives for more happiness with fewer possessions and less living space. In his TED Talk, *Less Stuff, More Happiness*, he shares an idea that we can still be happy with fewer things.

BEFORE VIEWING

A Read the following statements. Write **A** if you mostly agree or **D** if you mostly disagree. Then discuss your answers with a partner.

1. _____A_____ It is a good idea to stop buying things we don't really need.

2. _____A_____ Having less space makes life more difficult.

3. _____D_____ We don't really need most of the things that we own.

❝ I'm here to suggest . . . that less might actually equal more. **❞**

WHILE VIEWING

B ▶ **LISTEN FOR MAIN IDEAS** Watch Graham Hill's TED Talk. For each statement, write **A** if you think he would agree or **D** if you think he would disagree. Then discuss your answers with a partner.

1. _A_ It is a good idea to stop buying things.

2. _D_ Having less space makes life more difficult.

3. _A_ We don't really need most of the things that we own.

C ▶ **LISTEN FOR CAUSE AND EFFECT** Check (✓) the answers to the following questions. There may be more than one answer.

1. What are the trends that Hill described?

    a. ☑ People have much more space than they did 50 years ago.

    b. ☐ People today want things that are better in quality.

    c. ☑ People are turning to personal storage businesses to keep their stuff.

2. What are some of the effects of the trends Hill mentioned?

    a. ☑ money-related issues

    b. ☐ increased risk of business scams

    c. ☑ decreasing happiness levels

    d. ☑ negative impact on the environment

3. According to Hill, what are the benefits of having fewer things?

    a. ☐ a smaller carbon footprint

    b. ☑ saves money

    c. ☑ more freedom to do other things

    d. ☐ stronger relationships with other people

D ▶ **LISTEN FOR DETAILS** Watch Hill's TED Talk again. Complete the notes on the advice he gives for living with less.

---

1. Get rid of things ¹ _you don't need_. ² _think_ before you buy anything.

2. Make full use of the ³ _space_ that you have.

    e.g., stack things, ⁴ _digitize_ things like books and movies

3. Have ⁵ _multifuctional_ spaces and items.

    e.g., a sink + ⁶ _a toilet_, a dining table + ⁷ _a bed_

WORDS IN THE TALK

environmental footprint (n) the effect that a person, business, or activity has on the health of the planet

flat line (v) to remain the same; not increase

multi = more than one

AFTER VIEWING

E **ANALYZE METAPHORS** Hill says, "First of all, you have to edit ruthlessly. We've got to clear the arteries of our lives." What do the words "edit" and "arteries" normally mean? What do they refer to in the TED Talk? Complete the chart.

	Dictionary meaning	Meaning in the TED Talk
edit		
arteries		

F **APPLY** Work with a partner. Discuss the questions below.

1. How do you decide when you should buy something or let something go? Think of your own rule for each situation.

2. Do you agree with Hill's ideas for a happier life? What are some things in your life that you could apply these ideas to?

PRONUNCIATION *Intonation in Yes/No and Choice Questions*

G 🎧 Listen to the excerpts from the TED Talk. For each question, draw an arrow to indicate a rising or falling intonation.

1. "Is that really going to make me happier?"

2. "Could I do with a little life editing?"

3. "Would that give me a little more freedom?"

> **Pronunciation Skill**
>
> **Intonation in Yes/No and Choice Questions**
>
> Intonation is the way the voice rises and falls when speaking. In yes/no questions, the intonation usually rises at the end. In choice questions, where there are two or more options, the intonation rises on each choice, and falls on the last one.

H 🎧 Draw arrows to mark the intonation in each question. Listen and check your answers. Then practice saying them with a partner.

1. Would you like coffee?

2. Are you happier with more choices?

3. Would you like coffee or tea?

4. Is she going on vacation today?

5. Do you want to see a movie, play video games, or read a book?

I Write two yes/no questions and two choice questions. Then take turns asking and answering the questions with a partner.

Yes/No Question: _____

Yes/No Question: _____

Choice Question: _____

Choice Question: _____

Thinking Critically

ANALYZE INFORMATION

A Look at the infographic and answer the questions. Discuss your ideas with a partner.

1. What aspects does the Happy Planet Index measure? Why might it be more useful to include these instead of just one aspect?

2. What factors do you think people consider when they report their quality of life?

3. Look at the scores for the U.S.A. and Costa Rica. What is the main reason for the U.S.A.'s relatively low score?

4. How do you think your country would rate? Explain your reasons.

HAPPY PLANET INDEX

The Happy Planet Index (HPI) measures the degree to which people in each country live long, happy, sustainable lives. It is a combination of three measures:

LONGEVITY: the average age people are likely to live to

HAPPINESS: the quality of life they reported on a scale of 1–10

SUSTAINABILITY: their environmental footprint measured in gha (global hectares)

USA		Costa Rica
#122 OF 152	VS	#1 OF 152
HPI SCORE: 37.4		HPI SCORE: 62.1

LONGEVITY		
78.9 years		80.3 years

HAPPINESS		
6.9/10		7/10

SUSTAINABILITY		
8.2 gha		2.7 gha

Catarata del Toro waterfall in Costa Rica

Dancers in colorful costumes take part in the Independence Day parade in Quepos, Costa Rica.

B 🎧 Listen to a conversation about Costa Rica. What reasons does the man give for Costa Rica's global rankings in happiness and sustainability? Check (✓).

a. ☐ The country's economy is strong.

b. ☑ The people value the natural environment.

c. ☐ Costa Ricans live healthy lifestyles.

d. ☑ Costa Rica has great investment in education.

e. ☑ The people receive strong social support.

C Do you think a country's ranking in the Happy Planet Index is related to their overall level of happiness? In what ways might they be linked? Discuss with a partner.

COMMUNICATE   *Synthesize and evaluate ideas*

D What are some ways we can achieve happier, more sustainable lives? Compare the ideas from Lesson B's class discussion, Graham Hill's TED Talk, and the example of Costa Rica. Check (✓) the statements that apply to each person or example.

	A maximizer	A satisficer	Hill	Costa Rica
1. Buy things that will last for a long time				
2. Not everything can be perfect, but that's OK.				
3. Keep your carbon footprint small.				
4. Take time to review all available options before deciding.				
5. Spend time with friends and family.				

E Work in a group. Discuss the questions below.

1. Do you think Hill would encourage people to be a maximizer, a satisficer, or a bit of both? Why?

2. What are people in your country generally happy about? What are they less happy about?

3. In your opinion, what's the most important factor for personal happiness?

Putting It Together

LEARNING OBJECTIVES

- Research, plan, and present on the topic of achieving happier lives
- Use questions or stories to connect the ending of a talk to its beginning

ASSIGNMENT

Group presentation: Your group is going to give a presentation about the topic "less is more." Your presentation will address the question "Does having less make us happier?"

PREPARE

A Review the unit. In what way does each source below relate to the idea of "less is more"? Make notes in the chart.

The Paradox of Choice (Lesson B)	
Graham Hill (Lesson F)	
Happy Planet Index (Lesson G)	

B Work with your group. Choose one of the topics below or think of your own idea.

☐ Online streaming services offer a great range of choices.

☐ Supermarkets encourage us to buy more products than we really need.

☐ Your idea: _____

C Plan your presentation. Answer the questions about your topic in Exercise B. Make notes in the chart below.

Questions	Notes
What are some possible reasons for this?	
How do you feel about this? Why?	many options fun. conversation.
Do you want to see changes to this? If so, what are they? If not, why?	we want to many options ca vl.

D Look back at the vocabulary, pronunciation, and communication skills you've learned in this unit. What can you use in your presentation? Note any useful language below.

_____

_____

_____

_____

E Below are some ways to include a question or story in your presentation. Think about how you can connect the ending of your presentation to the beginning and add that to your plan.

Ask a question:

• _What do you think is . . .?_

• _What's the most important . . .?_

Tell a story:

• _A few years ago, I was . . ._

• _Someone told me that . . ._

> ### Presentation Skill
> **Connecting the Ending to the Beginning**
>
> Speakers sometimes end a presentation by referring back to something they said at the beginning. It can give a clear structure to your presentation. For example, you can ask a question or start a story at the beginning and answer the question or finish the story at the end. In Graham Hill's TED Talk, he begins by talking about the box on the stage and refers to it again at the end.

F Practice your presentation. Make use of the presentation skill that you've learned.

PRESENT

G Give your presentation to another group. Watch their presentation and evaluate them using the Presentation Scoring Rubrics at the back of the book.

H Discuss your evaluation with the other group. Give feedback on two things they did well and two areas for improvement.

Checkpoint

Reflect on what you have learned. Check your progress.

I can ... understand and use words to talk about the idea of minimalism.

amount	**bunch**	**digitize**	**disappear**	**ease**
equal	**majority**	**rarely**	**storage**	**stuff**

☐ use collocations with _amount_.

☐ watch and understand a talk about the idea of "less is more."

☐ use the correct intonation in yes/no and choice questions.

☐ interpret an infographic about the Happy Planet Index.

☐ synthesize and evaluate ideas about achieving happier lives.

☐ use questions or stories to connect the ending of a talk to its beginning.

☐ give a presentation on whether having less leads to greater happiness.

A family "city camping"
in Guangzhou, China.

8

Explore
Every Day

Q **How can we make
every day an
adventure?**

People often follow a daily routine, and
may think of an adventure as something
that's entirely different from their usual
activities. But, with a little creativity, we
can make our lives more interesting. In
this photo taken in Guangzhou, China,
a family is enjoying an unusual form of
camping—along a river in the city! In this
unit, we'll look at what creativity is, why it's
important, and how we can use creativity
to change and improve our everyday lives.

THINK and DISCUSS

1 Look at the photo and read the caption.
How do you feel about this activity? Would
you like to try it? Why, or why not?

2 Look at the essential question and the
unit introduction. What do you think the
connection is between adventure and
creativity?

Building Vocabulary

LEARN KEY WORDS

A  Listen to and read the information below. Do you think you were more creative when you were younger? Discuss with a partner.

Creativity and Age

Research on the relationship between creativity and age shows that we start out creative, but our level of creativity declines slowly as we age. This is less to do with the performance of the brain, and much more because of our behavior. As children, we are naturally **curious** about everything, and we learn through **observation**. We **search** for and **discover** new experiences, and our **minds** are open to new ideas. As we get older, we don't often **attempt** new things and tend to stick to familiar **solutions** to challenges. This may not be a choice: the **considerable** responsibilities we have as adults mean we are usually asked to be **productive** at the cost of being creative.

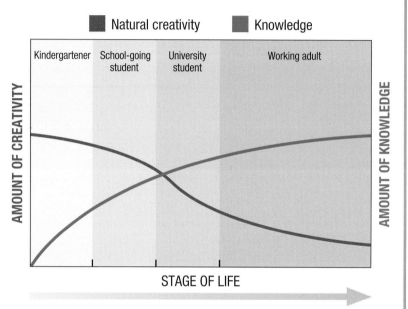

Natural creativity Knowledge

Kindergartener | School-going student | University student | Working adult

AMOUNT OF CREATIVITY

AMOUNT OF KNOWLEDGE

STAGE OF LIFE

Source: Jacek, F. Gieras, "Creativity and Innovations in the 21st Century" (2019)

B Match the correct form of each word in **bold** in Exercise A with its meaning.

1. _solutions_ a way to fix a problem
2. _search_ to look for something
3. _considerable_ large in number
4. _attempt_ to try to do something
5. _reserch_ the careful study of a subject to find new information about it
6. _minds_ a person's ability to think, feel, and understand things
7. _discover_ to find or learn about something for the first time
8. _observation_ the act of carefully watching something happen
9. _productive_ getting many things done or achieving good results
10. _curious_ interested in learning about things and people

C The words in the box collocate with the noun **research**. Complete the sentences using the correct form of the words.

scientific	show	base on	finding	carry out

1. We are planning to _show_ new research studying the effects of curiosity.

2. This latest research clearly _____ the importance of practicing creativity techniques.

3. Their research is _finding_ a very small sample and cannot be considered good evidence.

4. There is some interesting _scientific_ research on how music can boost creativity.

5. A team of psychologists presented their research _____ at the press conference.

D Complete the passage using the correct form of the words in **bold** from Exercise A.

There are many factors that can discourage creativity. Lack of discipline is one—it takes a disciplined
¹_____ to be creative, so developing a schedule that works for you will allow you to be
more ²_____. For example, plan to do any tasks that require creativity at a time of day
when you think most clearly. Impatience is another factor. Creativity takes time, so when looking for a
³_____ to a problem, try ⁴_____ for different possible ways of looking
at the issue. Fear of failure is also a common factor. However, ⁵_____ new things is
important for building creativity. Failure is a part of learning and can help you improve.

COMMUNICATE

E Work with a partner. Discuss the questions below.

1. How creative do you think you are? What are some examples of your creativity?

2. Do you think being more creative could help you in your daily life? How so?

Viewing and Note-taking

LEARNING OBJECTIVES

- Watch a lecture about creativity
- Review and reflect on your notes
- Make inferences using given information

BEFORE VIEWING

A 🎧 Listen to an explanation of the Cornell note-taking method. Label each section (1–3) in the template with the correct header.

> **Note-taking Skill**
>
> **Reviewing and Reflecting on Your Notes**
>
> Reviewing your notes and reflecting on what you have learned helps you better understand and remember information. Using the Cornell template, you can do this by looking at the questions and comments on your notes. Summarizing what you have learned encourages you to reflect and reinforces your learning.

Notes	Questions	Summary

1: _Questions_

2: _Notes_

Question

Observe

Network — to talk with different people

Experiment

Find connection — idea, problem, question

3: _Summary_

big idea, key idea

B 🎧 Listen to a talk and use the Cornell template in Exercise A to take notes in the "Notes" section.

C You are going to watch a lecture about creativity. What jobs require a lot of creativity? Are there any jobs where creativity is less important? Discuss with a partner.

WHILE VIEWING

D ▶ **LISTEN FOR MAIN IDEAS** Watch Segment 1 of the lecture. Choose the statement that best expresses the main idea.

a. Creativity skills should be developed from a young age.

b. The ability to be creative provides a range of benefits, including mental and physical health.

c. Studies show that artists and musicians have higher levels of creativity.

E ▶ **LISTEN FOR DETAILS** Watch Segment 2 of the lecture. Title each section and take notes in Sections 1 and 2.

1: _Questions_

discanpatness

expertise

2: _Notes_

~~was~~ 3 things of cleatie?

described need to creativity

1. expertise

2. creative thinking skill (solve problem)

3. motivation. (keep going)   all 3 : cleative + su ccess

3: _Summary_

F ▶ **SUMMARIZE** Watch Segment 2 again and review your notes in Exercise E. Summarize the segment in your own words in Section 3.

G **INFER** Use the information in the lecture to complete the inference statements below.

1. The speaker gives the examples of a scientist, a salesperson, and an office worker because ___C___.

   a. these jobs often have fixed routines

   b. these are some of the more common jobs people do

   c. these jobs seem to require skills and knowledge rather than creativity

2. When the speaker says that AI "is not yet good at being creative," she wants to point out that ___B___.

   a. AI can't do tasks that involve creativity

   b. creativity is still a valuable career skill

   c. AI is becoming more and more crucial for success in all kinds of businesses

> **Listening Skill**
>
> **Making Inferences**
>
> Speakers or writers don't always state something directly. However, there are often clues in the surrounding information to help you understand what the person is trying to say. When making an inference, ask yourself questions like "What information do I already know related to this?" or "Why did the speaker/writer say this?".

AFTER VIEWING

H **REFLECT** Work with a partner. Discuss the questions below.

1. Which of the five "creative" behaviors do you have? Which do you think you would want to practice doing?

2. Do you think it will be difficult to practice the five behaviors of being creative? Why, or why not?

UNIT 8

Noticing Language

LISTEN FOR LANGUAGE *Rephrase and summarize*

A Read the phrases below. Which ones are used for rephrasing and which are for summarizing? Write the title for each column.

Phrases for _____	Phrases for _____
in brief	in other words
in short	that is
to sum up	to put it another way
in the end	to put it simply

> **Communication Skill**
> **Rephrasing and Summarizing**
>
> When you explain or describe something, using other words to repeat your main points helps make the meaning clear to the listener. This is called rephrasing. At the end, it's useful to summarize or state your main ideas in one or two sentences. This shows the listener what you think is most important to remember.

B Listen to the following excerpts from the lecture in Lesson B. Complete the sentences with the words you hear.

1. ". . . being regularly involved in creative activities helps to reduce stress, results in greater satisfaction, and contributes to healthy aging. _____, creativity helps us lead longer, happier, and more productive lives.

2. "Experiment—_____, attempt new things, and change your normal routine."

3. "So, _____, creativity is vital—for our personal lives, our careers, and for our well-being and health."

C Look at the excerpts in Exercise B. Note in which excerpts (1–3) the speaker rephrases or summarizes her ideas.

Rephrasing: _____

Summarizing: _____

D Match the sentences with the most suitable rephrased or summarized statements (a–c).

1. _____ I need some help with an urgent design project.

2. _____ After using a rental car, clean the inside of the car and make sure that the gas tank is full.

3. _____ I need to submit a report to my manager by the end of the day, but I have not started on it yet.

a. To put it simply, I have to work late today.

b. In short, I'm looking for someone who's creative and able to work quickly.

c. In other words, make sure it is in a good condition before returning it.

A designer from Wooga works on a mobile game. Some of the company's most popular games are hidden object games.

E 🎧 Listen to a short talk about the creative success of Pixar. Choose the conclusion that best summarizes the talk.

    a. In short, Pixar believes it's important to let people build their own teams.

    b. To sum up, Pixar allows their employees to be their most creative selves by creating a comfortable work culture and environment.

    c. In conclusion, Pixar encourages creativity by giving people the freedom to plan their own work schedules.

F Check (✓) the principles or practices that were described in the talk. Then take turns explaining them to a partner in your own words.

    a. ☐ focus on people   **c.** ☐ set clear expectations

    b. ☐ allow constant feedback

COMMUNICATE

G Think of something you like that your partner may not know about: e.g., a movie, a book, or a video game. Think of details like the plot, the characters, or what's interesting or unique about it.

H Work with a partner. Take turns explaining your chosen topic. Describe what it is and how it works. Ask your partner follow-up questions when listening.

> So I'm really into this video game where the main character, a cat, has to explore an ancient city and solve a mystery in order to escape. In short, you're a cat who has to save the world.

> What can you do as that character?

Communicating Ideas

LEARNING OBJECTIVES

- Use appropriate language to rephrase and summarize the information received
- Collaborate to suggest ways to improve creativity skills

ASSIGNMENT

Task: You are going to collaborate in a group to discuss what each person would like to be more creative at and design a "creative routine" that could help improve their creativity skills.

LISTEN FOR INFORMATION

A 🎧 **LISTEN FOR MAIN IDEAS** Listen to three speakers talk about what creativity means to them. Then match the statements below with the speakers (1–3).

a. Speaker _____: Creativity is how we approach and solve a problem.

b. Speaker _____: Creativity begins only after other things are taken away to make space.

c. Speaker _____: Creativity consists of many small actions.

B 🎧 **LISTEN FOR DETAILS** Listen again. Which of the following best describes each speaker's routine? Check (✓).

	Speaker 1	Speaker 2	Speaker 3
I collect pictures of interesting places. They help me make the details in my designs look more realistic.			
I always ask my team members to look for ways of improving how we do things, instead of simply following the usual processes.			
I read different types of news every day and note down the popular topics. I also think about how to present these in a fun way.			

C Work with a partner. Which speaker's view of creativity do you agree with the most? Why?

COLLABORATE

D What would you personally like to be more creative at? Take turns sharing in a group. Take notes on each member's thoughts.

_____

_____

_____

A man rides an unusual bike on the street in Paris, France.

E As a group, come up with a "creative routine" or "creative habit" for each person. Think about an activity each person could add to their routine to build their creativity skills.

Name	Goal	Suggested creative routine/habit
	Get better at drawing	Draw one simple object every day

F Share your group's ideas with another group. Describe the "creative routines and habits" your group designed and how they might help each person improve their creativity skills.

Checkpoint

Reflect on what you have learned. Check your progress.

I can ...   understand and use words to talk about creativity.

attempt	**considerable**	**curious**	**discover**	**mind**
observation	**productive**	**research**	**search**	**solution**

use collocations with *research*.

watch and understand a lecture about creativity.

review and reflect on my notes.

make inferences based on given information.

notice language for rephrasing and summarizing information.

use language for rephrasing and summarizing information.

collaborate and communicate effectively to suggest ways of improving creativity skills.

A cyclist rides along a bicycle trail in the Turia Gardens in Valencia, Spain.

UNIT 8

E F G H

Building Vocabulary

LEARN KEY WORDS

A Listen to and read the passage below. How does your mood affect your creativity? When do you feel most creative? Discuss with a partner.

Creative Moods

How do our emotions affect our creativity? It's common to think of it in terms of positive and negative feelings, but psychologist Eddie Harmon-Jones suggests we should focus on how strong or weak these emotions are instead. **Based on** his team's research, weaker emotions, such as feeling relaxed or sad, can help us broaden our **imagination**. On the other hand, stronger emotions such as gratitude or anger can make us focus on achieving a goal. So depending on whether we want to **explore** new **possibilities** or develop an idea in detail, it may be more useful to get into a particular mood.

In reality, we're also usually not just happy or sad—we often feel a mix of emotions. And according to a study by Carnegie Mellon University, experiencing an unusual combination of emotions may help us think of unique ideas. This is probably why some companies like Disney and Google make their office spaces interesting—with gaming spaces and meeting rooms, employees aren't **trapped** at a regular office desk all the time. The unusual environments increase the chances of people experiencing different emotions at the same time, which leads to creative ideas!

So the next time you're looking for inspiration, try doing something **entirely** different from your usual activities or going somewhere you've never been.

B Work with a partner. Discuss the questions below.

1. How do you usually come up with ideas? Do you get inspiration from people or places around you?

2. Do you like exploring different ways of doing things? Or do you prefer doing something familiar? Why?

3. The photo on the previous page shows an urban park in Spain. What places do you often pass by on your way to school or work? How do those places make you feel?

C Match the correct form of each word in **bold** from Exercise A with its meaning.

1. _____ completely or definitely

2. _____ the mind's ability to think of different images and ideas

3. _____ a chance that something may happen in the future

4. _____ being unable to get free

5. _____ to look into and think about

6. _____ using certain ideas to make a decision

D Read the sentences below. Choose the correct meaning of the words in **bold**.

1. I cycle to school every day but even the fastest **route** takes me 45 minutes.

   a. a mode of transportation   **b.** a path to travel from one place to another

2. I love taking walks in the forest and being **surrounded** by tall trees, beautiful flowers, and the sounds of birds.

   a. to be above someone   **b.** to be everywhere around someone

3. The restaurant expanded its business and now has more than ten **locations** across the city.

   a. places   **b.** names

4. Action movies aren't really my favorite, but this one was **enjoyable**.

   a. fun and interesting   **b.** easy to understand

E The words in the box collocate with the noun **imagination**. Complete the sentences using the correct form of the words.

beyond	capture	stimulate	active

1. Young children tend to have _____ imaginations—they can see ordinary things in many different ways.

2. A change of scenery is often a good way to _____ our imagination.

3. The new bestselling novel series has really _____ the imagination of many around the world.

4. Before the Wright brothers developed the first airplane, many people thought flying was _____ imagination.

COMMUNICATE

F Think of an example for each prompt below. Make notes.

1. something that stimulates your imagination _____

2. an activity you find enjoyable _____

3. a scenic route you are familiar with _____

4. a great location for taking photos in your city _____

G Work with a partner. Take turns sharing your ideas in Exercise F. Respond to your partner's ideas or ask follow-up questions.

> What's something that stimulates your imagination?

> I think that reading fantasy novels helps stimulate my imagination because I can explore entirely new worlds.

UNIT 8

E F G H

Viewing and Note-taking

LEARNING OBJECTIVES

- Watch and understand a talk about a different way to explore places
- Notice the schwa sound in articles and prepositions

TEDTALKS

Daniele Quercia is a map researcher. He uses social media and large amounts of data to understand how people interact with their environment, both online and in the real world. In his TED Talk, *Happy Maps*, he shares an example of how this information helps make our lives happier and more satisfying.

BEFORE VIEWING

A The title of the TED Talk is *Happy Maps*. When do you use maps? What do you think a "happy map" is? Discuss with a partner.

" Einstein once said, 'Logic will get you from A to B. Imagination will take you everywhere.' **"**

PART 2 **155**

WHILE VIEWING

B ▶ **LISTEN FOR MAIN IDEAS** Watch Daniele Quercia's TED Talk. Choose the statement that best expresses his main idea.

a. Collecting personal data can improve maps.

b. Mobile mapping apps are likely to improve in the future.

c. You can make surprising discoveries by taking a different path.

C ▶ **SEQUENCE EVENTS** Watch Segment 1 of Quercia's TED Talk. Order the events below (1–7).

Quercia …

a. _5_ felt surprised.

b. _2_ moved to Boston.

c. _1_ finished his Ph.D. in London.

d. _7_ changed the focus of his research.

e. _6_ felt shame.

f. _4_ took a different route one day.

g. _3_ cycled to work every day.

D ▶ **LISTEN FOR DETAILS** Watch Segment 2 of Quercia's TED Talk. Choose the most suitable phrase or idea to complete each statement.

1. For their experiment, Quercia and his colleagues built a _c_ .

    a. bike path   **b.** web game   **c.** digital map

2. In the experiment, participants were asked to _a_ .

    a. choose the places that looked more quiet and beautiful

    b. vote for the best ways to travel through the city

    c. share photos of peaceful and beautiful places in their city

3. Quercia and his team found that _c_ .

    a. people preferred routes that were easy to travel

    b. not many people enjoy their commute

    c. people can travel a more enjoyable route without spending a lot more time

4. Quercia and his team's goal is to design a mapping tool that _c_ .

    a. shows people the places they love

    b. finds shorter routes that people don't know about

    c. suggests routes based on how they look, smell, and sound

---

WORDS IN THE TALK

aesthetics (n) sense of beauty
aggregate (v) combine; put together
cartography (n) mapmaking
crowdsourcing (n) getting support or ideas from a large number of people over the internet
data mining (n) computer analysis of large amounts of data to find patterns
Ph.D. (n) the highest college degree

E INFER Which of the following can we infer based on Quercia's TED Talk?
Check (✓). More than one answer is possible.

1. ☑ Quercia didn't enjoy his work commute.

2. ☑ Traditional mapping apps are great at saving people travel time.

3. ☑ Quercia believes traveling non-standard routes helps improve people's
experience of the city.

4. ☐ Quercia and his team's mapping tool doesn't calculate travel time.

5. ☐ Quercia and his team's mapping tool allows people to plan their journeys to
include places they love.

6. ☐ Quercia built his map as a way for people to share their experiences of the city
with family and friends.

AFTER VIEWING

F REFLECT Work with a partner. Discuss the questions below.

1. Do you think Quercia's map is useful in helping people explore the city? Why, or
why not?

2. Would you choose to spend more time traveling a "happy" path? Why, or why not?

PRONUNCIATION   *Schwa sound in articles and prepositions*

G 🎧 Listen to the excerpts below from the TED Talk. Complete the
sentences with the words with schwa sounds.

> **Pronunciation Skill**
>
> **Schwa Sound in Articles and Prepositions**
>
> In English, articles (*a, an, the*) and prepositions (*to, from, for*, etc.) are often pronounced with a schwa sound (/ə/), which can be difficult to hear in fast speech. Learning to listen for these schwa sounds helps you to get familiar with how English is naturally spoken.

1. "_____ few years ago, after finishing my Ph.D. in London,
I moved _____ Boston."

2. "... surprise _____ finding _____ street with no
cars."

3. "... we built _____ crowdsourcing platform, _____
web game."

4. "In tests, participants found _____ happy, _____
beautiful, _____ quiet path far more enjoyable
_____ shortest one."

H 🎧 Read the following sentences. Circle the articles and prepositions that have
schwa sounds. Then listen and check your answers.

1. A lot of people went to the party last week.

2. There's an art gallery at the top floor of the building.

3. I think there's a high chance of snow tonight.

4. She bought a cake for her classmate's birthday.

5. My closest friend is from the Philippines.

6. What kind of music do you like?

Thinking Critically

LEARNING OBJECTIVES

• Interpret an infographic about the daily routines of famous creative people
• Synthesize and evaluate ideas about creativity in everyday life

ANALYZE INFORMATION

A Look at the infographic and answer the questions. Discuss your ideas with a partner.

1. Which three things did the people spend the most time on?

2. Which three people spent the most time on creative work in a day?

3. Which person's routine did you find surprising or interesting? Why?

The Daily Routines of Famous Creative People

How do really creative people spend their days? The graph below shows the typical daily routines of some of the world's most famous people.

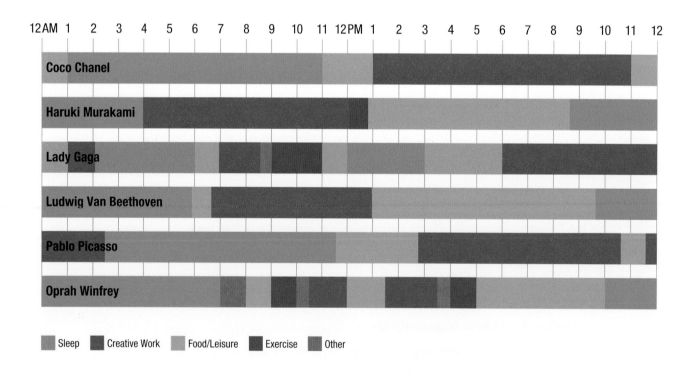

Sources: Mason Currey, *Daily Rituals: How Artists Work* (2013); Mason Currey, *Daily Rituals: Women at Work* (2019); Digital Information World; Podio

B How do you spend your day? Estimate the amount of time you usually spend on the activities below on a typical day. Then color the timeline accordingly. What do you spend the most time on? How often do you vary things?

■ Sleep: _____   ■ Exercise: _____

■ Creative Activities: _____   ■ Other: _____

■ Food/Leisure: _____

```
   12  1  2  3  4  5  6  7  8  9  10 11 12  1  2  3  4  5  6  7  8  9  10 11 12
   a.m.                                    p.m.
```

C 🎧 Listen to the podcast. Choose the statement that best summarizes the main idea.

a. Famous creative people have very different routines and ways of building their creativity.

b. Most people don't have the time or money to go on long, ambitious adventures.

c. Varying your routine by doing something different, like getting outside, encourages creativity.

D Work with a partner. Which of the activities from the podcast would you like to try to boost your creativity? Why?

- drawing some everyday objects
- writing a short poem about your day
- cooking something you know using new ingredients
- taking a different route home
- going on a microadventure

COMMUNICATE *Synthesize and evaluate ideas*

E How can Daniele Quercia's idea of "happy" maps and Alastair Humphreys's idea of microadventures help us be more creative in making our everyday lives fun? Work in a group and think of two microadventures you could do in your city using Quercia's mapping tool. Then share your ideas with another group.

Example: An aromatic walk

Walk home after school/work and take a path that smells nice. Walk along a street full of delicious food stores or walk through a park and enjoy the smell of the trees.

Adventure 1: _____

Adventure 2: _____

F Work with a partner. Discuss the questions below.

1. In addition to things like scenery and sounds that Quercia mentioned in his TED Talk, what factors do you think could be included in his "happy" maps? How do these improve people's travel experience?

2. Do you think microadventures are as meaningful as "traditional" adventures? Why, or why not?

Putting It Together

LEARNING OBJECTIVES

- Research, plan, and present on a personal adventure
- Use pauses to pace a presentation

ASSIGNMENT

Individual presentation: You are going to do a photography walk and give a presentation on your microadventure experience.

PREPARE

A Review the unit. How do the ideas below help improve creativity? Discuss with a partner.

Five creative behaviors (Lesson B)	"Happy" maps (Lesson F)	Microadventures (Lesson G)

B Choose one of the microadventures below. As you explore this new route, take pictures that match each of the descriptions in the chart below.

a. Take a different route home.

b. Travel on foot and visit somewhere local but new to you.

c. Cycle to a spot on your city map.

strange	soft	fast
amazing	MY PHOTOGRAPHY WALK	small
flat	bright	smelly

C Plan your presentation. Copy the chart above on a poster and stick your photos on it. Then make notes on the following questions.

1. What does each photo show? _____

_____

2. How does each photo match the description? _____

_____

3. How do you feel about this microadventure? _____

_____

D Look back at the vocabulary, pronunciation, and communication skills you've learned in this unit. What can you use in your presentation? Note any useful language below.

_____

_____

_____

_____

E Below are some tips for pacing your speech. Look back at your notes and consider how you can pace your presentation.

Before your presentation:

• Plan pauses in and between sentences, especially after important ideas.

• Record yourself speaking. Then listen to it and check your speed.

During your presentation:

• Pay attention to your audience when presenting, and slow down or speed up as needed.

> **Presentation Skill**
> **Pacing Your Presentation**
>
> Speaking clearly and at a regular pace during a presentation makes it easier for the audience to follow your ideas. Include short pauses where suitable. In Daniele Quercia's TED Talk, he often pauses after important ideas to give listeners more time to process and reflect on what they hear.

F Practice your presentation. Make use of the presentation skill that you've learned.

PRESENT

G Give your presentation to a partner. Watch their presentation and evaluate them using the Presentation Scoring Rubrics at the back of the book.

H Discuss your evaluation with your partner. Give feedback on two things they did well and two areas for improvement.

Checkpoint

Reflect on what you have learned. Check your progress.

I can ... ☐ understand and use words related to exploration and adventure.

| based on | enjoyable | entirely | explore | imagination |
| location | possibility | route | surrounded | trapped |

☐ use collocations with *imagination*.

☐ watch and understand a talk about a different way to explore places.

☐ notice the schwa sound in articles and prepositions.

☐ interpret an infographic about the daily routines of famous creative people.

☐ synthesize and evaluate ideas about creativity in everyday life.

☐ use pauses to pace my presentation.

☐ give a presentation on my experience of a microadventure.

Independent Student Handbook

The Independent Student Handbook is a resource you can use during and after this course. It provides additional support for listening, speaking, note-taking, pronunciation, presentation, and vocabulary skills.

LISTENING AND NOTE-TAKING

LISTENING STRATEGIES

Predicting

Speakers giving formal talks usually begin by introducing themselves and then introducing their topic. Listen carefully to the introduction of the topic and try to anticipate what you will hear.

Strategies:

- Use visual information including titles on the board, on slides, or in a PowerPoint presentation.
- Think about what you already know about the topic.
- Ask yourself questions that you think the speaker might answer, e.g., *What's the reason for A? How did B happen?*
- Listen for specific introduction phrases (see **Useful Phrases for Presenting**).

Listening for main ideas

It is often important to be able to tell the difference between a speaker's main ideas and supporting details.

Strategies:

- Listen carefully to the introduction. The main idea is often stated at the end of the introduction.
- Listen for rhetorical questions, or questions that the speaker asks and then answers. Often the answer is the main idea.
- Notice ideas that are repeated or rephrased. Repetition and rephrasing often signal main ideas (see **Useful Phrases for Presenting**).

Listening for details

Supporting details can be a name or a number, an example, or an explanation. When looking for a specific kind of information, it's useful to listen for words that are related to the information you need.

Strategies:

- Listen for specific phrases that introduce an example (see **Useful Phrases for Presenting**).
- Notice if an example comes after a general statement from the speaker or is leading into a general statement.
- Notice nouns that might signal causes/reasons (e.g., *factors, influences, causes, reasons*) or effects/results (e.g., *effects, results, outcomes, consequences*).
- Notice verbs that might signal causes/reasons (e.g., *contribute to, affect, influence, determine, produce, result in*) or effects/results (often these are passive, e.g., *is affected by*).
- Listen for specific phrases that introduce reasons/causes and effects/results (see **Useful Phrases for Presenting**).

Understanding the structure of the presentation

An organized speaker will use certain expressions to alert you to the important information that will follow. Notice signal words and phrases that tell you how the presentation is organized and the relationship between main ideas.

Introduction

A good introduction includes something like a thesis statement, which identifies the topic and gives an idea of how the lecture or presentation will be organized. Here are some expressions to listen for that indicate a speaker is introducing a topic (see also **Useful Phrases for Presenting**):

I'll be talking about …   *My topic is …*

There are basically two groups …   *There are three reasons …*

Body

In the body of the lecture, the speaker will usually expand upon the topic. The speaker will use phrases that tell you the order of events or subtopics and their relationship. Here are some expressions to listen for (see also **Useful Phrases for Presenting**):

The first/next/final (point) is …   *First/Next/Finally, let's look at …*

Another reason is …   *However, …*

Conclusion

In a conclusion, the speaker often summarizes what has been said and may discuss what it means, or make predictions or suggestions. Sometimes speakers ask a question to get the audience to think about the topic. Here are some expressions to listen for (see also **Useful Phrases for Presenting**):

In conclusion, …   *In summary, …*

As you can see …   *I/We would recommend …*

Understanding meaning from context

Speakers may use words that are new to you, or words that you may not fully understand. In these situations, you can guess the meaning by using the context or situation itself.

Strategies:

- Use context clues to guess the meaning of the word, then check if your guess makes sense. What does the speaker say before and after the unfamiliar word? What clues can help you guess the meaning of the word?

- Listen for words and phrases that signal a definition or explanation (see **Useful Phrases for Presenting**).

Recognizing a speaker's bias

It's important to know if a speaker is objective about the topic. Objective speakers do not express an opinion. Speakers who have a bias or strong feeling about the topic may express views that are subjective.

Strategies:

- Notice subjective adjectives, adverbs, and modals that the speaker uses (e.g., *ideal, horribly, should, shouldn't*). These suggest that the speaker has a bias.

- Listen to the speaker's tone. Do they sound excited, happy, or bored?

- When presenting another point of view on the topic, is that other point of view given much less time and attention by the speaker?

- Listen for words that signal opinions (see **Communication Strategies**).

NOTE-TAKING STRATEGIES

Taking notes is a personalized skill. It is important to develop a note-taking system that works well for you. However, there are some common strategies that you can use to improve your note-taking.

Before you listen

- Focus. Try to clear your mind before the speaker begins so you can pay attention. If possible, review previous notes or what you already know about the topic.

As you listen

Take notes by hand

Research suggests that taking notes by hand rather than on a laptop or tablet is more effective. Taking notes by hand requires you to summarize, rephrase, and synthesize the information. This helps you *encode* the information, or put it into a form that you can understand and remember.

Listen for signal words and phrases

Speakers often use signal words and phrases (see **Useful Phrases for Presenting**) to organize their ideas and indicate what they are going to talk about. Listening for signal words and phrases can help you decide what information to write down in your notes. For example:

Today we're going to talk about three alternative methods that are ecofriendly, fast, and efficient.

Condense (shorten) information

- As you listen, focus on the most important ideas. The speaker will usually repeat, define, explain, and/or give examples of these ideas. Take notes on these ideas.

    Speaker: *Worldwide, people are using and wasting huge amounts of plastic. For example, Americans throw away 35 million plastic bottles a year.*

    Notes: *Waste plastic, e.g., U.S. 35 mil plastic bottles/year*

- Don't write full sentences. Write only key words (nouns, verbs, adjectives), phrases, or short sentences.

    Full sentence: *The Maldives built a sea wall around the main island of Malé.*

    Notes: *Built sea wall—Malé*

- Leave out information that is unnecessary.

    Full sentence: *Van den Bercken fell in love with the music of Handel.*

    Notes: *VDB loves Handel*

- Write numbers and statistics (*35 mil; 91%*).
- Use abbreviations (*e.g., ft., min., yr*) and symbols (*=, ≠, >, <, %*).
- Use indenting. Write main ideas on the left side of the paper. Indent details.

    - *Benefits of car sharing*
        - *Save $*
            - *Saved $300-400/mo.*

- Write details under key terms to help you remember them.
- Write the definitions of important new words from the presentation.

After you listen

- Review your notes soon after the lecture or presentation. Add any details you missed.
- Clarify anything you don't understand in your notes with a classmate or teacher.
- Add or highlight main ideas. Cross out details that aren't important or necessary.
- Rewrite anything that is hard to read or understand. Rewrite your notes in an outline or other graphic organizer to record the information more clearly (see **Organizing Information**).
- Use arrows, boxes, diagrams, or other visual cues to show relationships between ideas.

Organizing information

Sometimes it is helpful to take notes using a graphic organizer. You can use one to take notes while you are listening or to organize your notes after you listen. Here are some examples of graphic organizers:

Flowcharts are used to show processes, or cause/effect relationships.

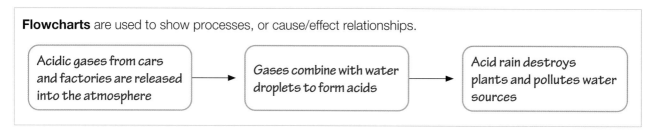

Mind maps show the connection between concepts. The main idea is usually in the center with supporting ideas and details around it.

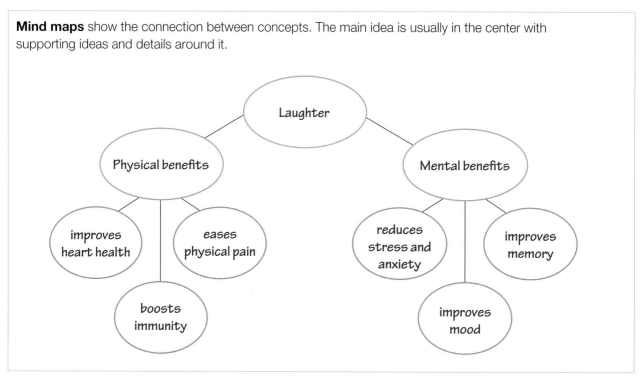

Outlines show the relationship between main ideas and details.

To use an outline for taking notes, write the main ideas starting at the left margin of your paper. Below the main ideas, indent and write the supporting ideas and details. You can do this as you listen, or go back and rewrite your notes as an outline later.

1. Saving Water
   A. Why is it crucial to save water?
      i. Save money
      ii. Not enough fresh water in the world

T-charts compare two topics.

Hands-On Learning	
Advantages	**Disadvantages**
1. Uses all the senses (sight, touch, etc.) 2. Encourages student participation 3. Helps memory	1. Requires many types of materials 2. May be more difficult to manage large classes 3. Requires more teacher time to prepare

Timelines show a sequence of events.

2002	2003	2005	2021
Graduated college	Got 1st job	Got promoted	Made vice president

Venn diagrams compare and contrast two or more topics. The overlapping areas show similarities.

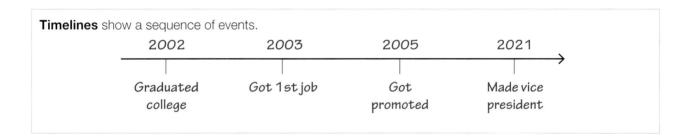

Skateboard   Microcar

All electric

Ebike

SPEAKING AND PRONUNCIATION

COMMUNICATION STRATEGIES

Successful communication requires cooperation from both the listener and speaker. In addition to verbal cues, the speaker can use gestures and other body language to convey their meaning. Similarly, the listener can use a range of verbal and non-verbal cues to show acknowledgment and interest, clarify meaning, and respond appropriately.

USEFUL PHRASES FOR EXPRESSING YOURSELF

The list below shows some common phrases for expressing ideas and opinions in class.

Expressing opinions

Your opinion is what you think or feel about something. You can add an adverb or adjective to make your statement stronger.

I think …   *If you ask me, …*
I feel …   *To me, …*
I'm sure …   *In my (honest) opinion/view …*
Personally, …   *I strongly believe …*

Expressing likes and dislikes

There are many expressions you can use to talk about your preferences other than *I like …* and *I don't like …* Using different expressions can help you sound less repetitive.

I enjoy …   *I can't stand …*
I prefer …   *I hate …*
I love …   *I really don't like …*
I don't mind …   *I don't care for …*

Giving facts

Using facts is a good and powerful way to support your ideas and opinions. Your listener will be more likely to believe and trust what you say.

There is evidence/proof …   *Researchers found …*
Experts claim/argue …   *The record shows …*
Studies show …

Giving tips or suggestions

There are direct and indirect ways of giving suggestions. Imperatives are very direct and let your listener know that it's important they follow your advice. Using questions can make advice sound less direct—it encourages your listener to consider your suggestion.

Direct   Indirect

Imperatives (e.g., Try to get more sleep.)   *It's probably a good idea to …*
You/We should/shouldn't …   *How about + (noun/gerund)*
You/We ought to …   *What about + (noun/gerund)*
I suggest (that) …   *Why don't we/you …*
Let's …   *You/We could …*

USEFUL PHRASES FOR INTERACTING WITH OTHERS

The list below shows some common phrases for interacting with your classmates during pair and group work exercises.

Agreeing and disagreeing

In a discussion, you will often need to say whether you agree or disagree with the ideas or opinions shared. It's also good to give reasons for why you agree or disagree.

Agree		Disagree
I agree.	*Definitely.*	*I disagree.*
True.	*Right!*	*I'm not so sure about that.*
Good point.	*I was just about to say that.*	*I don't know.*
Exactly.		*That's a good point, but I don't really agree.*
Absolutely.		*I see what you mean, but I think that ...*

Checking your understanding

To make sure that you understand what the speaker has said correctly, sometimes you might need to clarify what you hear. You can check your understanding by rephrasing what the speaker said or by asking for more information.

Are you saying that ... ?	*How so?*
So what you mean is ... ?	*I'm not sure I understand/follow.*
What do you mean?	*Do you mean ... ?*
How's that?	*I'm not sure what you mean.*

Clarifying your meaning

When listeners need to clarify what they hear or understand, speakers need to respond appropriately. Speakers can restate their main points or directly state implied main points.

What I mean by that is ...	*The point I'm making is that ...*
Not at all.	

Checking others' understanding

When presenting information that is new to listeners, it's good to ask questions to make sure that your listeners have understood what you said.

Does that make sense?	*Is that clear?*
Do you understand?	*Are you following me?*
Do you see what I mean?	*Do you have any questions?*

Asking for opinions

When we give an opinion or suggestion, it's good to ask other people for theirs, too. Ask questions to show your desire to hear from your listeners and encourage them to share their views.

What do you think?	*How do you feel?*
Do you have anything to add?	*What's your opinion?*
What are your thoughts?	*We haven't heard from you in a while.*

Taking turns

During a presentation or discussion, sometimes a listener might want to interrupt the speaker to ask a question or share their opinion. Using questions is a polite way of interrupting. However, the speaker may choose not to allow the interruption, especially if they are about to finish what they have to say.

<u>Interrupting</u>

Excuse me.
Pardon me.
Can I say something?
May I say something?
Could I add something?
Can I just say … ?
Can I stop you for a second?
Sorry to interrupt, but …

<u>Stopping others from interrupting</u>

Could I finish what I was saying?
If you'd allow me to finish …
Just one more thing.

<u>Continuing with your presentation</u>

May I continue?
Let me finish.
Let's get back to …

Asking for repetition

When a speaker speaks too fast or uses words that you are not familiar with, you might want the speaker to repeat themselves. You could apologize first, then politely ask the speaker to repeat what they said.

Could you say that again?
I'm sorry?
I didn't catch what you said.

I'm sorry. I missed that. What did you say?
Could you repeat that, please?

Showing interest

It's polite to show interest when you're having a conversation with someone. You can show interest by asking questions or using certain words and phrases. You can also use body language like nodding your head or smiling.

I see.　　　*Seriously?*　　*Wow.*
Good for you.　*Um-hmm.*　　*And? (Then what?)*
Really?　　　*No kidding!*　*That's funny/amazing/incredible/awful!*

PRONUNCIATION STRATEGIES

When speaking English, it's important to pay attention to the pronunciation of specific sounds. It is also important to learn how to use rhythm, stress, and pausing. Below are some tips about English pronunciation.

Specific sounds

Research suggests that clear pronunciation of consonant sounds (as compared to vowel sounds) is a lot more useful in helping listeners understand speech. This means that consonant sounds must be accurate for your speech to be clear and easy to understand. For example, /m/ and /n/ are two sounds that sound similar. In a pair of words like *mail* and *nail*, it is important to pronounce the consonant clearly so that the listener knows which word you are referring to.

But there are some exceptions. One example is the pair /ð/ and /θ/, as in *other* and *thing*. These are very often pronounced (both by first and second language English users) as /d/ and /t/ or /v/ and /f/ with little or no impact on intelligibility. There is a lot of variation in vowel sounds in Englishes around the world; however, these differences rarely lead to miscommunication.

Vowels			Consonants		
Symbol	Key Word	Pronunciation	Symbol	Key Word	Pronunciation
/ɑ/	hot	/hɑt/	/b/	boy	/bɔɪ/
	far	/fɑr/	/d/	day	/deɪ/
/æ/	cat	/kæt/	/dʒ/	just	/dʒʌst/
/aɪ/	fine	/faɪn/	/f/	face	/feɪs/
/aʊ/	house	/haʊs/	/g/	get	/gɛt/
/ɛ/	bed	/bɛd/	/h/	hat	/hæt/
/eɪ/	name	/neɪm/	/k/	car	/kɑr/
/i/	need	/nid/	/l/	light	/laɪt/
/ɪ/	sit	/sɪt/	/m/	my	/maɪ/
/oʊ/	go	/goʊ/	/n/	nine	/naɪn/
/ʊ/	book	/bʊk/	/ŋ/	sing	/sɪŋ/
/u/	boot	/but/	/p/	pen	/pɛn/
/ɔ/	dog	/dɔg/	/r/	right	/raɪt/
	four	/fɔr/	/s/	see	/si/
/ɔɪ/	toy	/tɔɪ/	/t/	tea	/ti/
/ʌ/	cup	/kʌp/	/tʃ/	cheap	/tʃip/
/ɛr/	bird	/bɛrd/	/v/	vote	/voʊt/
/ə/	about	/əˈbaʊt/	/w/	west	/wɛst/
	after	/ˈæftər/	/y/	yes	/yɛs/
			/z/	zoo	/zu/
			/ð/	they	/ðeɪ/
			/θ/	think	/θɪŋk/
			/ʃ/	shoe	/ʃu/
			/ʒ/	vision	/ˈvɪʒən/

Source: *The Newbury House Dictionary plus Grammar Reference*, Fifth Edition, National Geographic Learning/Cengage Learning, 2014.

Rhythm

The rhythm of English involves stress and pausing.

Stress

- English words are based on syllables—units of sound that include one vowel sound.
- In every word in English, one syllable has the strongest stress.
- In English, speakers group words that go together based on the meaning and context of the sentence. These groups of words are called *thought groups*. In each thought group, one word is stressed more than the others—the stress is placed on the stressed syllable in this word.
- In general, new ideas and information are stressed.

Pausing

- Pauses in English can be divided into two groups: long and short pauses.
- English speakers use long pauses to mark the conclusion of a thought, items in a list, or choices given.
- Short pauses are used between thought groups to break up the ideas in sentences into smaller, more manageable chunks of information.

Intonation

English speakers use intonation, or pitch (the rise and fall of their voice), to help express meaning. For example, speakers usually use a rising intonation at the end of *yes/no* questions, and a falling intonation at the end of *wh-* questions and statements.

PRESENTING

PRESENTATION STRATEGIES

The strategies below will help you to prepare, present, and reflect on your presentations.

Prepare

As you prepare your presentation:

Consider your topic

- *Choose a topic you feel passionate about.* If you are passionate about your topic, your audience will be more interested and excited about your topic, too. Focus on one major idea that you can bring to life. The best ideas are the ones your audience wants to experience.

Consider your purpose

- *Have a strong beginning.* Use an effective *hook*, such as a quote, an interesting example, a rhetorical question, or a powerful image to get your audience's attention. Include one sentence that explains what you will do in your presentation and why.

- *Stay focused.* Make sure your details and examples support your main points. Avoid sidetracks or unnecessary information that takes you away from your topic.

- *Use visuals that relate to your ideas.* Drawings, photos, video clips, infographics, charts, maps, slides, and physical objects can get your audience's attention and explain ideas effectively, quickly, and clearly. Slides with only key words and phrases can help emphasize your main points. Visuals should be bright, clear, and simple.

- *Have a strong conclusion.* A strong conclusion should serve the same purpose as the strong beginning—to get your audience's attention and make them think. Good conclusions often refer back to the introduction, or beginning, of the presentation. For example, if you ask a question in the beginning, you can answer it in the conclusion. Remember to restate your main points, and add a conclusion device such as a question, a call to action, or a quote.

Consider your audience

- *Share a personal story.* You can also present information that will get an emotional reaction; for example, information that will make your audience feel surprised, curious, worried, or upset. This will help your audience relate to you and your topic.

- *Use familiar concepts.* Think about the people in your audience. Ask yourself these questions: Where are they from? How old are they? What is their background? What do they already know about my topic? What information do I need to explain? Use language and concepts they will understand.

- *Be authentic (be yourself).* Write your presentation yourself. Use words that you know and are comfortable using.

Rehearse

- *Make an outline.* This will help you organize your ideas.

- *Write notes on notecards.* Do not write full sentences, just key words and phrases to help you remember important ideas. Mark the words you should stress and places to pause.

- *Check the pronunciation of words.* Review the pronunciation skills in your book. For words that you are uncertain about, check with a classmate or a teacher, or look them up in a dictionary. Note and practice the pronunciation of difficult words.

- *Memorize the introduction and conclusion.* Rehearse your presentation several times. Practice saying it out loud to yourself (perhaps in front of a mirror or video recorder) and in front of others.

- *Ask for feedback.* Use feedback and your own performance in rehearsal to help you revise your material. If specific words or phrases are still a problem, rephrase them.

Present

As you present:

- Pay attention to your pacing (how fast or slow you speak). Remember to speak slowly and clearly. Pause to allow your audience to process information.
- Speak at a volume loud enough to be heard by everyone in the audience, but not too loud. Ask the audience if your volume is OK at the beginning of your talk.
- Vary your intonation. Don't speak in the same tone throughout the talk. Your audience will be more interested if your voice rises and falls, speeds up and slows down to match the ideas you are talking about.
- Be friendly and relaxed with your audience. Remember to smile!
- Show enthusiasm for your topic. Use humor if appropriate.
- Have a relaxed body posture. Don't stand with your arms folded or look down at your notes. Use gestures when helpful to emphasize your points.
- Don't read directly from your notes. Use them to help you remember ideas.
- Don't look at or read from your visuals too much. Use them to support and illustrate your ideas.
- Make frequent eye contact with the entire audience.

Reflect

As you reflect on your presentation:

- Consider what you think went well during your presentation and what areas you can improve on.
- Get feedback from your classmates and teacher. How do their comments relate to your own thoughts about your presentation? Did they notice things you didn't? How can you use their feedback in your next presentation?

USEFUL PHRASES FOR PRESENTING

The chart below provides some common signposts and signal words and phrases that speakers use in the introduction, body, and conclusion of a presentation.

INTRODUCTION

Introducing a topic

I'm going to talk about …
My topic is …
I'm going to present …
I plan to discuss …
Let's start with …
Today we're going to talk about …

So we're going to show you …
Now/Right/So/Well, (pause) let's look at …
There are three groups/reasons/effects/factors …
There are four steps in this process.

BODY

Listing or sequencing

First/First of all/The first (noun)/To start/To begin, …
Second/Secondly/The second/Next/Another/Also/ Then/In addition, …
Last/The last/Finally …
There are many/several/three types/kinds of/ways, …

Signaling problems/solutions

The problem/issue/challenge (with …) is …
One solution/answer/response is …

Giving reasons or causes	**Giving results or effects**
Because + (clause): Because it makes me feel happy …	*so + (clause): so I decided to try photography*
Because of + (noun phrase): Because of climate change …	*Therefore, + (sentence): Therefore, I changed my diet.*
Due to + (noun phrase) …	*As a result, + (sentence).*
Since + (clause) …	*Consequently, + (sentence).*
The reason that I like video games is …	*… causes + (noun phrase)*
One reason that people do surveys is …	*… leads to + (noun phrase)*
One factor is + (noun phrase) …	*… had an impact/effect on + (noun phrase)*
The main reason that …	*If … then …*
Giving examples	**Repeating and rephrasing**
The first example is…	*What you need to know is …*
Here's an example of what I mean …	*I'll say this again, …*
For instance, …	*So again, let me repeat …*
For example, …	*The most important point is …*
Let me give you an example …	
… such as …	
… like …	
Signaling additional examples or ideas	**Signaling to stop taking notes**
Not only … but	*You don't need this for the test.*
Besides …	*This information is in your books/on your handout/ on the website.*
Not only do … but also	*You don't have to write all this down.*
Identifying a side track	**Returning to a previous topic**
This is off-topic, …	*Getting back to our previous discussion, …*
On a different subject, …	*To return to our earlier topic …*
As an aside, …	*OK, getting back on topic …*
That reminds me ….	*So to return to what we were saying, …*
Signaling a definition	**Talking about visuals**
Which means …	*This graph/infographic/diagram shows/explains …*
What that means is …	*The line/box/image represents …*
Or …	*The main point of this visual is …*
In other words, …	*You can see …*
Another way to say that is …	*From this we can see …*
That is …	
That is to say …	

CONCLUSION

Concluding	
Well/So, that's how I see it.	*As you can see, …*
In conclusion, …	*At the end, …*
In summary, …	*To review, + (restatement of main points)*
To sum up, …	

BUILDING VOCABULARY

VOCABULARY LEARNING STRATEGIES

Vocabulary learning is an ongoing process. The strategies below will help you learn and remember new vocabulary.

Guessing meaning from context

You can often guess the meaning of an unfamiliar word by looking at or listening to the words and sentences around it. Speakers usually know when a word is unfamiliar to the audience, or is essential to understanding the main ideas, and will often provide clues to its meaning.

- Restatement or synonyms: A speaker may give a synonym to explain the meaning of a word, using phrases such as *in other words, also called, or ...,* and *also known as.*
- Antonyms: A speaker may define a word by explaining what it is NOT. The speaker might say *unlike A, ...,* or *in contrast to A, B is ...*
- Definitions: Listen for signals such as *which means* or *is defined as*. Definitions can also be signaled by a pause.
- Examples: A speaker may provide examples that can help you figure out what something is. For example, *Paris-Plage is a **recreation** area on the River Seine, in Paris, France. It has a sandy beach, a swimming pool, and areas for inline skating, playing volleyball, and other activities.*

Understanding word families: stems, prefixes, and suffixes

Use your understanding of stems, prefixes, and suffixes to recognize unfamiliar words and to expand your vocabulary. A stem is the root part of the word, which provides the main meaning.

A prefix is before the stem and usually modifies meaning (e.g., adding *re-* to a word means "again"). A suffix is after the stem and usually changes the part of speech (e.g., adding *-ation/-sion/-ion* to a verb changes it to a noun). For example, in the word *endangered*, the stem or root is *danger*, the prefix is *en-*, and the suffix is *-ed*. Words that share the same stem or root belong to the same word family (e.g., *event, eventful, uneventful, uneventfully*).

Word Stem	Meaning	Examples
ann (or *enn*)	year	anniversary, millennium
chron(o)	time	chronological, synchronize
flex (or *flect*)	bend	flexible, reflection
graph	draw, write	graphics, paragraph
lab	work	labor, collaborate
mob	move	mobility, automobile
sect	cut	sector, bisect
vac	empty	vacant, evacuate

Prefix	Meaning	Examples
auto-	self	automatic, autonomy
bi-	two	bilingual, bicycle
dis-	not, negation, remove	disappear, disadvantage
inter-	between	internet, international
mis-	bad, badly, incorrectly	misunderstand, misjudge
pre-	before	prehistoric, preheat
re-	again, back	repeat, return
trans-	across, beyond	transfer, translate

Suffix	Part of speech	Examples
-able (or *-ible*)	adjective	believable, impossible
-en	verb	lengthen, strengthen
-ful	adjective	beautiful, successful
-ize	verb	modernize, summarize
-ly	adverb; adjective	carefully, happily; friendly, lonely
-ment	noun	assignment, statement
-tion (or *-sion*)	noun	education, occasion
-wards	adverb	backwards, forwards

Using a dictionary

A dictionary is a useful tool to help you understand unfamiliar vocabulary you read or hear. Here are some tips for using a dictionary:

- When you see or hear a new word, try to guess its part of speech (noun, verb, adjective, etc.) and meaning, then look it up in a dictionary.

- Some words have multiple meanings. Look up a new word in the dictionary and try to choose the correct meaning for the context. Then see if it makes sense within the context.

- When you look up a word, look at all the definitions to see if there is a basic core meaning. This will help you understand the word when it is used in a different context. Also look at all the related words or words in the same family. This can help you expand your vocabulary. For example, the core meaning of *structure* involves something built or put together.

struc·ture /ˈstrʌktʃər/ *n.* **1** [C] a building of any kind: *A new structure is being built on the corner.* **2** [C] any architectural object of any kind: *The Eiffel Tower is a famous Parisian structure.* **3** [U] the way parts are put together or organized: *the structure of a song‖a business's structure*
—*v.* [T] **-tured, -turing, -tures** to put together or organize parts of s.t.: *We are structuring a plan to hire new teachers.* **-adj. structural.**

Source: *The Newbury House Dictionary plus Grammar Reference,* Fifth Edition, National Geographic Learning/Cengage Learning, 2014.

Multi-word units

You can improve your fluency if you learn and use vocabulary as multi-word units: idioms (*mend fences*), collocations (*trial and error*), and fixed expressions (*in other words*). Some multi-word units can only be understood as a chunk—the individual words do not add up to the same overall meaning. Keep track of multi-word units in a notebook or on note cards.

Collocations

A collocation is two or more words that often go together. A good way to sound more natural and fluent is to learn and remember as many collocations as you can. Look out for collocations as you read a new text or watch a presentation. Then note them down and try to use them when speaking or in your presentation.

You can organize your notes in a chart to make it easier to review and add to the list as you learn more collocations:

share an have an ask for change your	*opinion(s)*
fulfill manage set exceed	*expectation(s)*
encounter	problems resistance obstacles difficulty

Vocabulary note cards

You can expand your vocabulary by using vocabulary note cards. Write the word, expression, or sentence that you want to learn on one side. On the other, draw a four-square grid and write the following information in the squares: definition, translation (in your first language), sample sentence, synonyms. Choose words that are high frequency or on the academic word list. If you have looked a word up a few times, you should make a card for it.

definition:	*first language translation:*
sample sentence:	*synonyms:*

Organize the cards in review sets so you can practice them. Don't put words that are similar in spelling or meaning in the same review set, as you may get them mixed up. Go through the cards and test yourself on the meanings of the words or expressions. You can also practice with a partner.

Presentation Scoring Rubrics

Unit 1

Presenter(s): _____

The presenter(s) …

	Fair 😊	**Good** 😄	**Excellent!** 😃
started the presentation in an engaging way.			
presented information in a logical sequence that is easy to follow.			
spoke clearly with appropriate pacing, volume, and intonation.			
included details and examples about the community project.			
concluded by explaining why the project will be helpful.			
What did you like?	1. 2.		
What could be improved?	1. 2.		

Unit 2

Presenter(s): _____

The presenter(s) …

	Fair 😊	**Good** 😄	**Excellent!** 😃
presented information in a logical sequence that is easy to follow.			
spoke clearly with appropriate pacing, volume, and intonation.			
used repetition to emphasize important ideas.			
described the kinds of career expectations their interviewee faced.			
described how their interviewee managed those expectations.			
What did you like?	1. 2.		
What could be improved?	1. 2.		

Unit 3

Presenter(s): _____

The presenter(s) ...

	Fair ☺	Good 😄	Excellent! 😆
presented information in a logical sequence that is easy to follow.			
spoke clearly with appropriate pacing, volume, and intonation.			
connected with the audience.			
identified two areas the government should spend more money in.			
provided reasons and evidence to support their ideas.			
What did you like?	1. 2.		
What could be improved?	1. 2.		

Unit 4

Presenter(s): _____

The presenter(s) ...

	Fair ☺	Good 😄	Excellent! 😆
presented information in a logical sequence that is easy to follow.			
spoke clearly with appropriate pacing, volume, and intonation.			
used adverbs to emphasize important points.			
gave three recommendations for setting realistic goals.			
included details and examples of each recommendation.			
What did you like?	1. 2.		
What could be improved?	1. 2.		

Unit 5

Presenter(s): _____

The presenter(s) …

	Fair ☺	Good 😄	Excellent! 😆
presented information in a logical sequence that is easy to follow.			
spoke clearly with appropriate pacing, volume, and intonation.			
described their community's approach to an environmental problem.			
suggested a way to improve the measure(s).			
concluded the presentation with a strong ending.			
What did you like?	1. 2.		
What could be improved?	1. 2.		

Unit 6

Presenter(s): _____

The presenter(s) …

	Fair ☺	Good 😄	Excellent! 😆
presented information in a logical sequence that is easy to follow.			
spoke clearly with appropriate pacing, volume, and intonation.			
explained key terms or concepts.			
described a cybercrime that happened in real life.			
explained how people can protect themselves from the cybercrime.			
What did you like?	1. 2.		
What could be improved?	1. 2.		

Unit 7

Presenter(s): _____

The presenter(s) ...

	Fair ☺	Good ☻	Excellent! ☺
presented information in a logical sequence that is easy to follow.			
spoke clearly with appropriate pacing, volume, and intonation.			
gave possible reasons for the business's behavior.			
expressed their view on whether "less is more."			
connected the end of the presentation with the beginning.			
What did you like?	1. 2.		
What could be improved?	1. 2.		

Unit 8

Presenter(s): _____

The presenter(s) ...

	Fair ☺	Good ☻	Excellent! ☺
presented information in a logical sequence that is easy to follow.			
spoke clearly with appropriate volume and intonation.			
used pauses to pace their presentation.			
described the photos and explained what they meant.			
described how they felt about the photography walk.			
What did you like?	1. 2.		
What could be improved?	1. 2.		

Vocabulary Index

Word	Unit	CEFR	Word	Unit	CEFR	Word	Unit	CEFR
absence	5	B2	employer	6	B1	productive	8	B2
account	6	B1	encouraging	3	B1	professional	6	B1
achieve*	4	B1	energy*	4	B1	promote*	3	B2
admire	3	B1	enjoyable	8	B1	protect	5	B1
alive	1	B1	enthusiastic	3	B2	proud	2	B1
ambitious	4	B2	entirely	8	B2	quit	4	B1
amount	7	B1	equal	7	B1	rarely	7	B1
anonymously	1	-	establish*	4	B2	realistic	2	B1
anxiety	1	B2	expectation	2	B2	reduce	5	B1
attachment*	6	B2	explore	8	B1	reflect	1	B2
attempt	8	B1	extension	6	B2	reject*	2	B2
attraction	3	B1	extreme	5	B2	remain	2	B1
aware of*	2	B2	familiar	7	B1	remind	1	B1
balance	4	B2	financial*	3	B1	require*	5	B1
based on	8	B2	flood	5	B1	research*	8	B1
behavior	4	B1	focus*	4	B2	response*	1	B2
blame	2	B1	force	3	B2	rise	5	B1
budget	3	B2	freedom	7	B2	risk	2	B2
bunch	7	B1	generate*	3	B2	route*	8	B1
carbon	5	B2	get into	4	C1	routine	4	B1
careless	6	B1	global*	5	B2	salary	2	B1
challenging*	4	B1	happiness	7	B1	satisfied	7	B1
choice	2	B1	identity*	6	B2	search	8	B1
choose	7	A1	imagination	8	B1	secret	1	B1
collection	1	B1	increase	6	B1	shocking	1	B1
comment*	6	B1	individual*	7	B1	silly	1	B1
commitment*	4	B2	influence	3	B2	similar*	1	B1
community*	1	B2	invest*	3	B2	society	3	B1
conflict*	2	B2	involve*	2	B1	solution	8	B1
connection	1	B1	land	5	B1	spirit	1	B2
considerable*	8	B1	likely	7	B1	spread	1	B2
control	3	B1	link*	6	B1	storage	7	B1
create*	1	B1	location*	8	B1	stranger	1	B1
creativity*	3	B2	loss	5	B2	stress*	4	B1
crime	6	B1	majority*	7	B2	struggle	4	B2
criminal	6	B1	manage	2	B1	stuff	7	B1
curious	8	B1	massive	5	B2	suffer	5	B2
current	5	B2	matter	2	A2	suggest	4	B1
data*	6	B2	melt	5	B2	support	3	B1
decision	7	B1	military*	3	B2	surround	8	B1
demonstrate*	3	B2	mind	8	B1	thought	1	B1
depend on	2	B1	motivation*	4	B2	trail	6	B2
desire	4	B2	observation	8	B2	trap	8	B2
development	5	B1	option*	7	B1	trust	2	B1
digital	6	A2	ordinary	5	B1	user	6	B1
digitize	7	-	personal	6	B1	value	3	B1
disappear	7	B1	plenty	4	B1	variety	7	A2
disappointed	2	B1	possibility	8	B1	visible*	6	B2
discover	8	B1	post	6	A2	vision*	2	B2
earn a living	2	B2	power	3	B1	willing	4	B1
ease	7	B2	predict*	5	B1	witness	5	B2
economic*	3	B2	preserve	1	B2	work out	2	B2
effect	5	B1	privacy	6	B2			
effort	4	B1	private	1	B1			

*These words are on the Academic Word List (AWL). The AWL is a list of the 570 most frequent word families in academic texts. It does not include the most frequent 2,000 words of English.

Credits

Cover Tampatra1/Dreamstime.com, **iii** (from top to bottom, left to right) © James Duncan Davidson/
TED, South China Morning Post/Getty Images, © TED Conferences LLC, © Blake Farrington, © Marla
Aufmuth/TED, © Kris Krug, © James Duncan Davidson/TED, © TED Conferences LLC, **iv** (from top to
bottom) Jasmine Clarke/The New York Times/Redux, Karen Moskowitz/Stone/Getty Images, Future
Publishing/Getty Images, Sylvain Lefevre/Getty Images Sport/Getty Images, Steve McCurry/Magnum
Photos New York, Gunnar Knechtel/laif/Redux, Tony Anderson/DigitalVision/Getty Images, © Zhou
Dainan, **2–3** Jasmine Clarke/The New York Times/Redux, **4** (c) MediaNews Group/Orange County
Register/Getty Images, (br) Cengage Learning, **6** © Candy Chang, **7** (cl) (c) (cr) SolStock/E+/Getty Images,
9 Norman Eggert/Alamy Stock Photo, **10** ProjectUA/Shutterstock.com, **12** The Asahi Shimbun/Getty
Images, **15** © James Duncan Davidson/TED, **18** Cengage Learning, **19** Hill Street Studios/DigitalVision/
Getty Images, **22–23** Karen Moskowitz/Stone/Getty Images, **24** MoMo Productions/DigitalVision/
Getty Images, **26** Edwin Tan/Getty Images, **28** Oliver Rossi/Stone/Getty Images, **32** © Vincent Fournier,
35 South China Morning Post/Getty Images, **38** (bkg) Andresr/E+/Getty Images, (bl) Cengage Learning,
42–43 Future Publishing/Getty Images, **44** (bkg) Saiko3p/Shutterstock.com, (bl) Christophe Testi/
Shutterstock.com, **46** Galitskaya/iStock/Getty Images, **49** Xinhua News Agency/Getty Images, **50** © Bruno
Morandi/Robert Harding Library, **52** Christopher Pillitz/Hulton Archive/Getty Images, **54** Quim Llenas/
Getty Images Entertainment/Getty Images, **55** © TED Conferences LLC, **58** (bkg) Farbregas Hareluya/
Shutterstock.com, (c) Cengage Learning, **59** Klaus Vedfelt/DigitalVision/Getty Images, **62–63** Sylvain
Lefevre/Getty Images Sport/Getty Images, **64** (bkg) © Anastasia Taylor-Lind, (cr) Cengage Learning,
65 Cengage Learning, **66** Chris Schmidt/E+/Getty Images, **69** Gregg Vignal/Alamy Stock Photo, **72** Angela
Weiss/AFP/Getty Images, **75** © Blake Farrington, **76** Buda Mendes/Getty Images News/Getty Images,
78 (bkg) ArtistGNDphotography/E+/Getty Images, (br) Cengage Learning, **79** Ethan Miller/Getty Images
North America/Getty Images, **82–83** Steve McCurry/Magnum Photos New York, **84** (bkg) Wildart/E+/
Getty Images, (cr) Cengage Learning, **87** Emmanuel Dunand/AFP/Getty Images, **89** SLSK Photography/
Shutterstock.com, **90** Sunsetman/Shutterstock.com, **92** © Frans Lanting/National Geographic Image
Collection, **95** © Marla Aufmuth/TED, **98** (c) Cengage Learning, (br1) StudioU/DigitalVision Vectors/
Getty Images, (br2) Rambo182/DigitalVision Vectors/Getty Images, **99** Jeremy Sutton-hibbert/Alamy
Stock Photo, **102–103** Gunnar Knechtel/laif/Redux, **104** (bkg) Dragon Images/Shutterstock.com,
(br) Cengage Learning, **107** D3sign/Moment/Getty Images, **109** Luis Alvarez/DigitalVision/Getty Images,
112 Michael Gottschalk/Getty Images News/Getty Images, **115** © Kris Krug, **117** Alvaro Gonzalez/
Moment/Getty Images, **118** Westend61/Getty Images, **122–123** Tony Anderson/DigitalVision/Getty
Images, **124** (bl) Cengage Learning, (r) FangXiaNuo/E+/Getty Images, **126** Uli Seit/The New York Times/
Redux, **129** Agefotostock/Alamy Stock Photo, **131** Monkey Business Images/Shutterstock.com,
132 Artparadigm/DigitalVision/Getty Images, **135** © James Duncan Davidson/TED, **138** (bkg) Miroslav_1/
iStock/Getty Images, (br) Christophe Testi/Shutterstock.com, **139** Cara Koch/Alamy Stock Photo,
142–143 © Zhou Dainan, **144** (cr) Cengage Learning, (b) South_agency/E+/Getty Images, **146** SeventyFour/
Shutterstock.com, **149** Dpa picture alliance archive/Alamy Stock Photo, **151** Kavalenkava Volha/Alamy
Stock Photo, **152** Cum Okolo/Alamy Stock Photo, **155** © TED Conferences LLC, **158** Cengage Learning,
162 © Jared Soares, **178–181** stas11/Shutterstock.com

Acknowledgments

The authors and publisher would like to thank the following teachers from all over the world for their valuable input during the development process of *21st Century Communication*, Second Edition.

Adriana Baiardi, Colegio Fatima; **Anouchka Rachelson**, Miami Dade College; **Ariya Kilpatrick**, Bellevue College; **Beth Steinbach**, Austin Community College; **Bill Hodges**, University of Guelph; **Carl Vollmer**, Ritsumeikan Uji Junior and Senior High School; **Carol Chan**, National TsingHua University; **Dalit Berkowitz**, Los Angeles City College; **David A. Isaacs**, Hokuriku University; **David Goodman**, National Kaohsiung University of Hospitality and Tourism; **Diana Ord**, Emily Griffith Technical School; **Elizabeth Rodacker**, Bakersfield College; **Emily Brown**, Hillsborough Community College; **Erin Frederickson**, Macomb Community College; **George Rowe**, Bellevue College; **Heba Elhadary**, Gulf University for Science and Technology; **Kaoru Lisa Silverman**, Kyushu Sangyo University; **Lu-Chun Lin**, National Yang Ming Chiao Tung University; **Madison Griffin**, American River College; **Mahmoud Salman**, Global Bilingual Academy; **Marta O. Dmytrenko-Ahrabian**, Wayne State University; **Michael G. Klüg**, Wayne State University; **Monica Courtney**, LaGuardia Community College; **Nora Frisch**, Truckee Meadows Community College; **Pamela Smart-Smith**, Virginia Tech; **Paula González y González**, Colegio Mar del Plata Day School; **Richard Alishio**, North Seattle College; **Rocío Tanzola**, Words; **Shaoyun Ma**, National TsingHua University; **Sorrell Yue**, Fukuoka University; **Susumu Onodera**, Hirosaki University; **Xinyue Hu**, Chongqing No. 2 Foreign Language School; **Yi Shan Tsai**, Golden Apple Language Institute; **Yohei Murayama**, Kagoshima University